# TRUE OR FALSE?

This person can make the dead tell secrets. ➞

# TRUE!

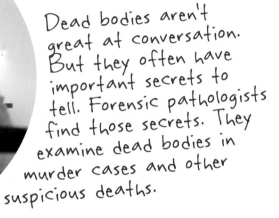

Dead bodies aren't great at conversation. But they often have important secrets to tell. Forensic pathologists find those secrets. They examine dead bodies in murder cases and other suspicious deaths.

It's not a pretty job. Bodies arrive with ID tags on their toes. Pathologists look inside their stomachs. They check under fingernails. They poke at livers and kidneys. They test body fluids.

If they're lucky, they find out how, why, and when a person died. Secrets like that can help put a murderer in jail.

Book design by Red Herring Design/NYC

Copyright © 2007 by Scholastic Inc.
All rights reserved. Published by Scholastic Inc.
Printed in the U.S.A.

ISBN-13: 978-0-545-34951-2
ISBN-10: 0-545-34951-6
(meets NASTA specifications)

6  7  8  9  10        113        20  19  18  17  16  15  14

# TOE TAGGED

## True Stories From the Morgue

Jaime Joyce

**WARNING:** This book involves real-life murder cases. Some of the cases may be disturbing—like the ones that involve cutting open dead bodies. And that would be all of them!

SCHOLASTIC INC.
New York  Toronto  London  Auckland
Sydney  New Delhi  Hong Kong

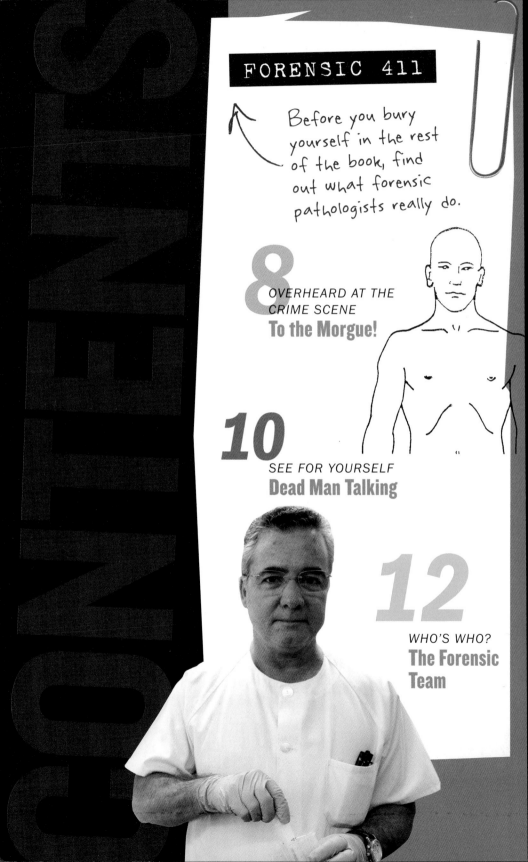

These cases are 100% real. Find out how forensic pathologists solved two murder mysteries.

**15**

### Case #1:
### Murder in Philly

A young woman drowns in the bathtub. Is it an accident? Or is it murder? Can a forensic autopsy help investigators solve the mystery?

A young woman is found dead in a Philadelphia suburb.

**29**

### Case #2:
### Rush to Judgment

Forensic experts go to great lengths to prove a man's innocence.

Was a woman pushed down some stairs in Shelburne, Nova Scotia?

# FORENSIC DOWNLOAD

Examine this! Here's even more amazing stuff about forensic pathology.

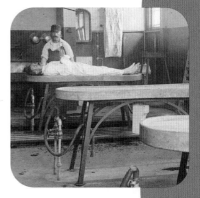

## YELLOW PAGES

Every murderer leaves behind one important clue: the victim's body.

## FORENSIC 411

It's a forensic pathologist's job to find the evidence. When did the victim die? What caused the death? Was there foul play? The answers to these questions lie beneath the skin—and under the fingernails and in the blood.

IN THIS SECTION:

- ▶ how FORENSIC PATHOLOGISTS really talk;
- ▶ what they look for on a DEAD BODY;
- ▶ whom they work with at the CRIME SCENE.

# To the Morgue!

**Forensic pathologists have their own way of speaking. Find out what their vocabulary means.**

"Did someone call the medical examiner? We need a doctor here at the crime scene."

**medical examiner** (MED-uh-kul eg-ZAM-uh-nur) a doctor who directs the examination of bodies in murder cases and other suspicious deaths; also called *ME*

**homicide** (HOM-uh-side) murder; the killing of one human being by another

"I may not be an expert, but I think we're dealing with a homicide. How accidental can ten stab wounds be?"

**morgue** (morg) a place where dead bodies are examined and stored

**autopsy** (AW-top-see) a complete examination of a dead body. An autopsy is done to determine how and when a person has died.

"Let's get the body back to the morgue for an autopsy."

The Greek word "autopsia" means "to see with one's own eyes."

8

"Call in a forensic pathologist. We're going to need a specialist's help."

## Say What?

Here's some other lingo a forensic pathologist might use on the job.

**forensic pathologist**
(fuh-REN-zick path-OHL-uh-jist) a doctor who examines dead bodies for evidence to be used in court

*"Patho" means "disease, suffering." "Ologist" means "someone who studies."*

**clinical autopsy**
(KLIN-uh-kul AW-top-see) an autopsy done on someone who has died of natural causes
*"You've got the wrong lab. This is the crime lab. We don't handle **clinical autopsies**."*

**coroner**
(KOR-uh-ner) an elected official who investigates sudden and unnatural deaths
*"Call the **coroner**. There's no hope for this guy."*

"Let me know when the forensic autopsy results are in. I want to know if I have the evidence to arrest this guy."

**exhume**
(eg-ZOOM) to dig up a dead body
*"I wish they had done an autopsy before the burial. Now we have to **exhume** him."*

**forensic autopsy**
(fuh-REN-zick AW-top-see) the examination of a body for evidence in a court case

**foul play**
(fowl play) an act or instance of criminal violence
*"This case was no accident. It feels like **foul play** to me."*

9

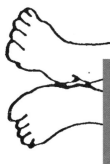

Are there any broken bones? That could indicate foul play.

Are the **victim**'s nails broken? That could mean that there was a struggle. And skin or blood found under nails can be tested to see if it matches a **suspect**.

Are there cuts, bruises, or scrapes on the skin? Pathologists study them for clues. The size of a stab wound, for example, could relate to the size of the killer's knife.

Urine from the bladder is taken to test for drugs.

# Dead Man Talking

**Every dead body has a story to tell. It takes a forensic pathologist to make sure its voice is heard.**

A body is found and no one knows why the person died. Was it murder? Suicide? A strange hidden illness? these, police call in a forensic **pathologist**. The pathologist performs an autopsy to answer

The kidneys and liver are examined to see if the victim was beaten. Pathologists also test these organs for poison.

Air passages might show traces of soot from a fire or water from a drowning.

Does the body have tattoos or birthmarks? These marks can help police identify the body.

c

Is there food in the stomach? Is it fully digested? The answers can help determine time of death.

Tiny red marks in the whites of the eyes could be a sign that the person was strangled.

Plastic bags are placed over the hands until the autopsy so that **evidence** won't be lost.

**1. What is the manner of death?** This question has five possible answers. The manner of death could be natural, accidental, homicide, suicide, or undetermined.

**2. What is the cause of death?** Cause of death is more specific than manner of death. It has to do with exactly how the person died. For example, in a homicide the cause of death could be a gunshot wound, stabbing, poisoning—or something else.

**3. When did the person die?** The answer can help catch a suspect in a lie. (See Case #1.)

How does the body help answer these questions? Take a look at the diagram above, and you'll see. (Then, if you still have the stomach for it, turn to page 48 for a step-by-step guide to an autopsy.)

# The Forensic Team

**Forensic pathologists work as part of a team. Here's a look at some of the experts who help solve crimes.**

### FORENSIC PATHOLOGISTS
They examine bodies for clues in murder cases and other suspicious deaths.

### FORENSIC NURSES
They help with autopsies. They collect, preserve, and document evidence found on the body.

### DETECTIVES OR AGENTS
They direct the crime investigation. They collect information about the crime, interview witnesses, identify suspects—and arrest them if there's enough evidence!

### DIENERS
They work in morgues and help with autopsies. They weigh and measure bodies. They also help to confirm a dead person's identity.

### FORENSIC TOXICOLOGISTS
They're called in to test victims for drugs, alcohol, and/or poison.

### MEDICAL EXAMINERS
They're medical doctors who investigate suspicious deaths. They try to find out when and how someone died. They often direct other members of the team.

# TRUE-LIFE CASE FILES!

**24 hours a day, 7 days a week, 365 days a year, forensic pathologists are solving mysteries.**

**Here's how forensic pathologists get the job done.**

What does it take to solve a crime? Good forensic pathologists don't just make guesses. They're scientists. They follow a step-by-step process.

As you read the case studies, you can follow along with them. Keep an eye out for the icons below. They'll clue you in to each step along the way.

 **THE QUESTION** At the beginning of a case, pathologists identify **one or two main questions** they have to answer.

 **THE EVIDENCE** The next step is to **gather and analyze evidence**. What was the person's medical history? What can be observed on the body? Pathologists study the answers to find out what they mean.

 **THE CONCLUSION** Along the way, they come up with theories to explain how, when, and why a person died. They test these theories against the medical evidence. Does the evidence back up the theory? **If so, they've reached a conclusion**. And chances are, they've come up with evidence that could help crack the case.

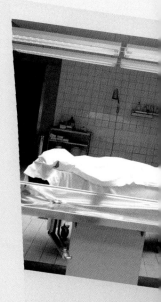

Merion, Pennsylvania
April 30, 1997
12:39 A.M.

# Murder in Philly

A young woman drowns in the bathtub.
Is it an accident? Or is it murder? Can
a forensic autopsy help investigators
solve the mystery?

# Death in the Bathtub

**Police get a panicked 911 call. Craig Rabinowitz says his wife has drowned in the bath.**

Stefanie Rabinowitz seemed to have it all. She had a successful law career. She lived in a wealthy suburb of Philadelphia. She had a loving husband and a beautiful one-year-old daughter.

Then, at age 29, it all came to an end in a terrible accident. Or so it seemed.

Craig Rabinowitz made the call in the early morning hours of April 30, 1997. A 911 operator answered the phone. Craig sounded panicked. His wife was in the bathtub, he said. She wasn't moving and he couldn't wake her up.

Stefanie Rabinowitz was just 29 years old when she died in her own bathtub.

Police arrived within minutes. Craig showed them upstairs to the bathroom. There, still in the tub, lay Stefanie's lifeless body. She wore a watch, a ring, and some other jewelry. Medical technicians tried to revive her. But Stefanie was already dead.

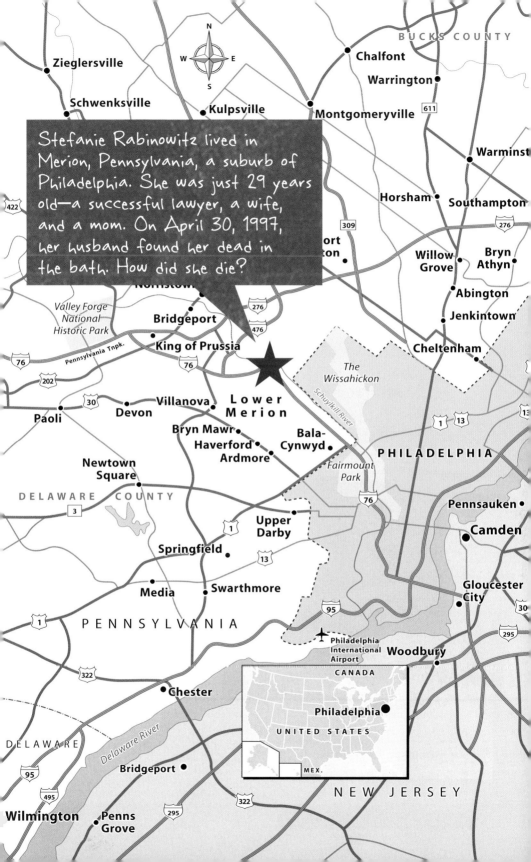

Stefanie Rabinowitz lived in Merion, Pennsylvania, a suburb of Philadelphia. She was just 29 years old—a successful lawyer, a wife, and a mom. On April 30, 1997, her husband found her dead in the bath. How did she die?

The police wondered, What could have caused her sudden death? Craig had been home watching TV, he said. He found his wife dead in the bath around midnight. Could someone have sneaked in and killed Stefanie? Police searched the home for signs of forced entry. No windows were open. All the doors were locked. Had Stefanie Rabinowitz simply drowned? Did she slip and hit her head in the bathtub? To police, that seemed like the best explanation.

Stefanie's body was removed from the home. It was taken to Halbert Fillinger, the Montgomery County coroner. Fillinger would decide whether an autopsy was needed.

By the time medical technicians arrived, Stefanie Rabinowitz was dead. Her body was taken to the coroner's office.

# WHO'S IN CHARGE HERE?

## Coroners? Medical examiners? Forensic pathologists? What's the difference?

**L**ike many smaller communities, Montgomery County didn't have its own medical examiner. The coroner had to send Stefanie Rabinowitz's body to Philadelphia for an autopsy. Here's who does what.

**Coroners** are usually elected or appointed. In most states, and in some parts of Canada, they do not have to be doctors. They sign death certificates. They generally do not perform autopsies.

**Medical examiners** are required to be doctors. In some states they need training in forensic pathology as well.

**Forensic pathologists** are doctors who are specially trained to investigate cases of sudden, violent, and unexpected death.

# The Husband's Story

## Detectives bring Craig Rabinowitz in for questioning.

Craig Rabinowitz, Stefanie's husband, claimed he was watching TV just before he found his wife, dead.

The next day, Craig Rabinowitz met with detectives. He arrived at the Lower Merion Township police station at 6 P.M. Two officers questioned him for about an hour. They wanted to know exactly what happened the night Stefanie died.

Craig recalled the entire night for the detectives. He and Stefanie had eaten at a Chinese restaurant. They got home at around 7:30, he said. Then he took their daughter, Haley, for a walk. He and Haley were back by 8:00.

At 11 P.M., Craig said, he was in the bedroom, watching a hockey game on TV. Stefanie was in the bathroom. She was getting ready for bed. At around 11:45, Craig heard a thump.

"I had heard it a thousand times," he said. "It was when the shampoo falls off the holder."

"How much time was there from the thump until you went in and found Stefanie?" the detectives asked.

"Thirty-five minutes," Craig said.

Craig told the two detectives that he tried to pull Stefanie from the tub. "I don't know why, I just couldn't get her out," he said.

Just before Craig left, detectives asked him a final question. Did he have life insurance on his wife? Craig

According to Craig Rabinowitz, it was 11.45 P.M. when he heard a noise from the bathroom.

Craig Rabinowitz had a life insurance policy on his wife. Detectives wondered if he killed her to collect this money.

said yes. He could collect more than a million dollars after Stefanie's death.

Could Craig have murdered his wife for the money?

The detectives needed more information about Craig. They also needed an autopsy report.

# Signs of Struggle

**Does Stefanie Rabinowitz's body hold clues to the mystery of her death?**

Halbert Fillinger didn't need to know about the life insurance. As coroner, he was in charge of Stefanie Rabinowitz's body. And he was already suspicious. Stefanie was young. She was healthy. No one had witnessed her death. To Fillinger, it didn't sound like an accident. He ordered an autopsy. Stefanie's funeral would have to wait.

Dr. Ian Hood, Philadelphia's deputy medical examiner, or **ME**, performed the autopsy. He knew that police initially thought Stefanie's death was an accident. He also knew that Fillinger thought it might be murder. As a forensic pathologist, Dr. Hood knew how to tell the difference.

What was the manner and cause of death? Hood was determined to find out.

The doctor began the autopsy with an external exam. He looked for bruises, cuts, and other marks on Stefanie's body.

It didn't take long to find evidence of a struggle. Around Stefanie's neck, Hood discovered some scrapes. The skin had been rubbed away. He also found tiny red marks on the inside of Stefanie's eyelids.

Next, Hood began the internal exam. He found undigested food in Stefanie's stomach. The food was still recognizable. Hood decided it was shrimp and bean sprouts.

So far, the clues pointed toward homicide. But Hood needed more evidence. He ordered a **toxicology** test to see if Stefanie had drugs in her system when she died. When the results came in, he would make his report.

**[Forensic Fact]**
Tissue samples are usually stored for 3–5 years after a forensic autopsy. In cases of suspicious death they can be stored longer.

## DRUG TEST
### Experts can find signs of poison in a body long after death.

In every autopsy, experts test the body for drugs or poisons. The tests are done in a toxicology lab. Toxicologists can test tissue from an organ, blood, and urine.

Pathologists usually collect a sample during the autopsy. They send the sample to the lab for testing.

The toxicologist tries to determine three things: What kind of drug was used, if any? How was it taken (through the mouth, a needle, etc.)? When was it taken? The answers help an ME or pathologist decide how and when a person died.

# The Body Talks

### What did Dr. Hood learn from the autopsy?

Hood considered the evidence. The marks on Stefanie's neck looked like they had been made by human hands. The tiny red spots on the eyelids were **hemorrhages**. A hemorrhage is caused when a blood vessel bursts inside the body. Strangling tends to burst blood vessels in the eyes of the victim.

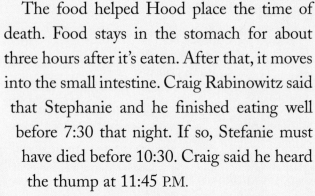

Tests showed that Stefanie Rabinowitz had a big dose of sleeping pills in her system when she died.

The food helped Hood place the time of death. Food stays in the stomach for about three hours after it's eaten. After that, it moves into the small intestine. Craig Rabinowitz said that Stephanie and he finished eating well before 7:30 that night. If so, Stefanie must have died before 10:30. Craig said he heard the thump at 11:45 P.M.

When the toxicology results came in, Hood had everything he needed. The tests showed traces of a sleeping pill called Ambien in Stefanie's blood. She had twice the normal dose in her system.

The results were clear: Stefanie's death was not accidental. Dr. Hood ruled her death a homicide. The cause of death was "manual strangulation." Stefanie's killer had choked her with his own hands.

**[Forensic Fact]**
Homicide is the sixth-leading cause of death in the United States. Ten percent of deaths in the U.S. each year are the result of homicide.

# Busted!

## With the autopsy report in hand, police close in on Craig Rabinowitz.

Stefanie's autopsy results came as a shock to her family. Craig insisted he was innocent. But police felt sure he had killed his wife. On May 5, 1997, they arrested Craig Rabinowitz and charged him with murder. His daughter, Haley, went to live with Stefanie's mother. Less than a week had passed since his wife's death.

With Craig Rabinowitz under arrest, police searched the suspect's home. They found business records and receipts. The papers showed that Rabinowitz was deeply in debt. They also looked at phone records. They discovered that he was involved with another woman.

As police dug further, the evidence piled up. Craig Rabinowitz had bought the life insurance policy on his wife just a few months earlier. Police also checked pharmacy records. Craig had a prescription for Ambien. That's the powerful sleeping pill that was found in

When police searched the Rabinowitz home, they discovered financial records. The couple was deeply in debt.

Stefanie's body. Rabinowitz had bought a new bottle of pills the day before Stefanie died.

By the fall, lawyers for the county were ready to go to court.

# Case Closed

**Craig goes to trial—then to prison for life.**

On October 30, 1997, Craig Rabinowitz appeared in court. He was charged with murdering his wife. Everyone was ready for a long and difficult trial.

But Rabinowitz ended the trial before it began. He told the court that he had recently had a dream. In the dream, he was in the house he grew up in. Three dead loved ones were there: his father, his father-in-law, and his wife. The three said to him, "Craig, it's time to do what's right."

Rabinowitz decided to follow the advice. He admitted to killing his wife. He had drugged Stefanie. While she slept, he choked her with his bare hands. Then he put her in the tub to make it look like she had drowned. He did it to get the insurance money so he could pay off his debts.

The judge sentenced Craig to life in prison. Rabinowitz was led from the courtroom. Before he left, he tried to explain what he had done. "I lost the ability to know right from wrong," he confessed. **24/7**

Craig Rabinowitz appeared in court on October 30, 1997. He was accused of murdering his wife, and during his trial, he confessed to the crime. He was sentenced to life in prison.

# DR. AUTOPSY

## Dr. Michael Baden has performed more than 20,000 autopsies.

**Y**ou may know him as the guy on the HBO series *Autopsy*. But important government agencies like the Federal Bureau of Investigation (FBI) know him as the guy to call to find out how someone died.

Dr. Baden has been a medical examiner for more than 45 years. Now, in addition to hosting his TV show, Dr. Baden is a forensic pathologist for the New York State Police. "If someone dies in jail or custody or on the highway," Baden told crimelibrary.com, "I'm available to explain what happened."

### Old Mysteries

Dr. Baden also uses new forensic techniques to investigate old mysteries. In the 1990s, he examined the body of slain civil rights leader Medgar Evers. Baden found evidence that led to the conviction of Evers's murderer.

Baden was also involved in examining remains that may have belonged to the last royal family in Russia, the Romanovs. The Romanovs were shot in 1918. Baden traveled to Russia to identify their remains in 1992.

### A Career in Autopsies

Like all forensic pathologists, Dr. Baden went to medical school. But he points out that there are many jobs in forensic science that don't require a medical degree. He advises young people, "You should inquire of your local police departments as to their standards for employment."

For Dr. Baden, this kind of work is extremely rewarding. There are very few forensic pathologists in the country, he explains. If he didn't do this work, it may not get done. He told crimelibrary.com, "Most satisfying to me is being able to explain to family members what happened to their loved one."

In this case, a woman died in suspicious circumstances —and her husband turned out to be the murderer. In the next case, another woman dies in a mysterious accident. Will her husband, too, prove to be the killer?

# Rush to Judgment

Shelburne, Nova Scotia,
Canada
February 20, 1989

**Forensic experts go to
great lengths to prove
a man's innocence.**

# A Fatal Fall

**A woman tumbles down a flight of stairs and dies at the hospital.**

At first, it looked like a terrible accident. On February 20, 1989, Janice Johnson lay at the bottom of her basement steps. Blood spread out slowly around her. She was barely conscious. She struggled for air.

It was 7:51 A.M. in the small town of Shelburne, Nova Scotia. Janice's neighbor, Robert Molloy, had just arrived to drop off his daughter. Janice was supposed to babysit. Her husband, Clayton, and their two daughters had already left for the day.

Janice Johnson was rushed to the hospital after she was discovered at the bottom of a flight of stairs.

When Molloy saw Janice, he ran to call for an ambulance. Medical workers arrived within minutes. They tried desperately to save the bleeding woman. She was rushed to the hospital, barely alive.

At 8:11 A.M., Clayton Johnson arrived at the school where he taught industrial arts. A secretary told him to get to the hospital right away. He arrived just before his wife died.

Clayton Johnson spent 15 minutes alone with his wife's body. Then he helped police piece together what had happened.

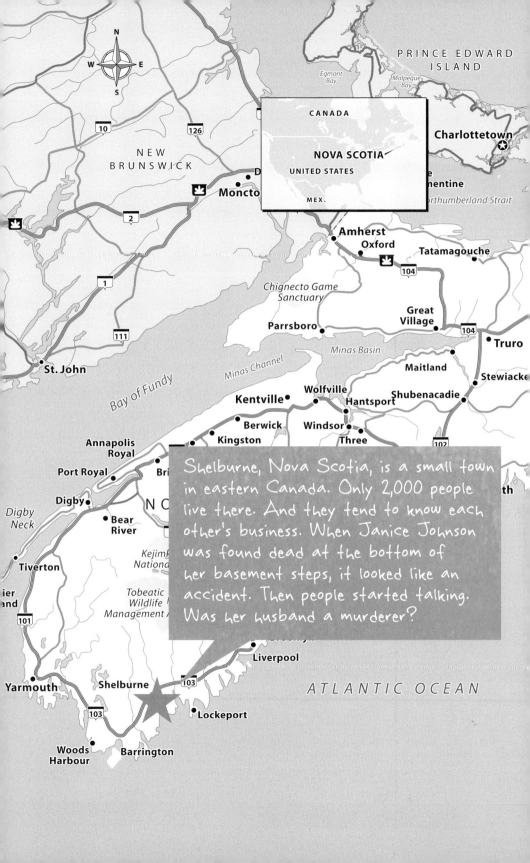

PRINCE EDWARD ISLAND

CANADA

NOVA SCOTIA

UNITED STATES

MEX.

Charlottetown

Egmont Bay

Malpeque Bay

NEW BRUNSWICK

Moncto

Amherst
Oxford
Tatamagouche

nentine

orthumberland Strait

Chignecto Game Sanctuary

Great Village

Parrsboro

Truro

Minas Basin

Maitland

Stewiacke

St. John

Bay of Fundy

Minas Channel

Wolfville

Kentville

Hantsport

Shubenacadie

Berwick

Windsor

Annapolis Royal

Kingston

Three

Port Royal

Bri

Digby

N

Digby Neck

Bear River

Kejim
Nationa

Tiverton

Tobeatic
Wildlife
Management A

er
and

Shelburne, Nova Scotia, is a small town in eastern Canada. Only 2,000 people live there. And they tend to know each other's business. When Janice Johnson was found dead at the bottom of her basement steps, it looked like an accident. Then people started talking. Was her husband a murderer?

Liverpool

ATLANTIC OCEAN

Yarmouth

Shelburne

Lockeport

Woods Harbour

Barrington

Clayton Johnson insisted that he had nothing to do with his wife's death.

At 7 A.M., Clayton Johnson had called Molloy. He asked Molloy to bring his daughter over at 8:00.

At 7:40, Clayton watched his two daughters get on the school bus. He left for work a few minutes later. When he kissed his wife good-bye, she was on the phone with a friend. Her brother was supposed to visit any minute. And Robert Molloy would be there soon.

Then Janice Johnson must have fallen down the steps. The accident happened between about 7:45 and 7:51 in the morning.

But was Clayton Johnson telling the truth?

# Open and Shut Case

**Clayton Johnson's story is confirmed by witnesses—and the body of his wife.**

Police checked out Clayton Johnson's story. They talked to the friend who called Janice Johnson that morning. She said she heard Clayton's voice over the phone. He said, "See you later, hon." Then she heard a kissing sound. That was about 7:45 A.M.

Police also talked to other people around town. Several friends had seen Clayton Johnson driving to work that morning. He stopped for gas. He drove slowly behind a school bus for several miles. He made the 16-mile (26-km) trip by 8:11. Police figured he must have left by 7:45. His wife's phone conversation ended shortly after. Malloy arrived at 7:51.

How could Clayton possibly have murdered his wife? He had only three or four minutes to kill her, hide the weapon, clean himself up, and leave for work. He knew people would be arriving soon. Why would he choose that morning to do it?

Janice Johnson's skull had been crushed in an accidental fall. That's what had killed her, coroner Roland Perry decided.

Roland Perry didn't think Clayton Johnson was a murderer. Perry was the chief coroner of Nova Scotia. He performed the autopsy on Janice Johnson. He didn't see any signs of a struggle. There were no bruises on her hands or arms.

Perry decided that Janice Johnson had died from a severe head injury. Her skull had been crushed. The right side of

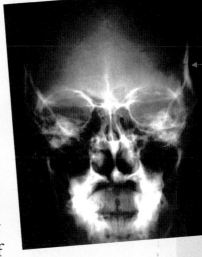

An officer from the Royal Canadian Mounted Police reenacts what Coroner Perry thought happened to Janice Johnson. First, she fell down the stairs, and her head landed in a gap.

her head showed a deep wound. The other side had smaller scrapes.

Perry studied photos of the Johnson home. The position of the body was hard to explain. Janice lay on her back at the bottom of the stairs. One leg rested on the bottom step. Had she turned in midair as she fell?

It wasn't a perfect explanation. But everything else pointed to an accidental death. The bloodstains were around her body. If Janice Johnson had been beaten, blood would have spattered on the walls.

Perry also noticed a five-inch (13-cm) gap between the stairs and the basement wall. He concluded that Janice Johnson had been a victim of terrible luck. She slipped on something at the top of the steps. When she fell, her head landed in the gap. The force crushed her skull.

Coroner Perry filled out a **death certificate** for Janice Johnson. He said the death was an accident.

Clayton Johnson was left to care for his daughters in peace.

Then, according to Coroner Perry, Janice Johnson's body flipped around. She landed on the floor, facing up. Later, some people would point out that this theory seemed very unlikely.

# Questioning the Coroner

**A new investigation puts Clayton Johnson in the spotlight.**

On one point, everyone agreed: Clayton Johnson had suffered a terrible loss. But as the seasons changed, so did public opinion.

Three months after his wife's death, Johnson began dating again. His new girlfriend, Tina Weybret, was 22. Johnson was 52.

People in town began to talk. It was too soon for Johnson to start dating, they thought. In a year, the couple was married. Had their relationship started before Janice's death?

Before long, a police corporal named Brian Oldford overheard the gossip. He started to investigate. Had Tina Weybret been a **motive** for murder?

Oldford also learned Clayton had $125,000 in life insurance on his wife. Clayton had bought the policy just months before she died. But Oldford overlooked an important fact. At that time, teachers in Nova Scotia were offered a new insurance plan. Almost *half* of them bought a new policy at that time!

Oldford then found two women who had helped clean the basement after Janice Johnson's death. He showed them photos of their friend's body. Suddenly, the women recalled seeing blood spattered on the walls of the basement. They had said nothing about the stains when they first talked to police.

Oldford called in two forensic pathologists, Charles Hutton and David King. He shared the new information with them. The men discussed the story about the blood **spatters**. They came up with a theory. There had probably been a struggle. Someone had hit Janice Johnson on the head. The murder weapon was probably a baseball bat or a wooden board, they said.

Oldford gave his new findings to Coroner Perry. Perry decided to change Janice Johnson's death certificate. He said her death was a homicide—a murder!

In April 1992, police arrested Clayton Johnson. He went to trial for first-degree murder. The judge warned the **jury** that the case against Johnson was weak. But on May 4, 1993, the jurors found Johnson guilty. He was sentenced to 25 years in prison.

Was it justice? In May 1993, a jury decided that Clayton Johnson was guilty of murder.

## FOR THE RECORD

**Every death has paperwork to go with it.**

Everyone gets a certificate at birth. It lists all the important details: your name; your parents' names; and when and where you were born.

A similar thing happens when you die. A death certificate lists the date and time of a person's death. It also lists the manner and cause of death.

When a hospital patient dies, the hospital tells the coroner or medical examiner. The coroner or medical examiner issues the death certificate. If the cause of death is not clear, it's the coroner's or ME's job to order an autopsy.

In this case, the coroner, Roland Perry, performed the first autopsy on Janice Johnson.

# Seeking Justice

**From behind bars, Clayton Johnson reaches out for help.**

Clayton Johnson tried to appeal his case twice. He was turned down both times. In 1995, he got some help. A group called the Association in Defense of the Wrongly Convicted agreed to investigate his case.

Lawyers James Lockyer and Phil Campbell worked for free. They set out to prove that Johnson was innocent. Their most important evidence would come from several pathologists. One of them was Dr. Linda Norton, who works in Dallas, Texas.

THE QUESTION

Could Dr. Norton figure out once and for all how Janice Johnson died?

THE EVIDENCE

Norton examined all the evidence. She looked at photographs of the Johnson home and of Janice's body. She read the police report, hospital records, and Perry's autopsy report.

After considering the facts, Dr. Norton agreed with Dr. Perry. Janice Johnson's death had been an accident. But Dr. Norton did not agree with Dr. Perry's theory about *how* Janice had fallen.

THE CONCLUSION

"I think I was in the shower when it hit me," Dr. Norton recalls. "Wait a minute," she thought. "Suppose Janice fell backward?" This would explain the position of the body at the bottom of the stairs. It would also explain a bruise on the back of Johnson's leg.

Lockyer and Campbell wanted to test Norton's theory. They contacted Dr. Herb MacDonell. MacDonell is a blood spatter **expert**. He runs the Laboratory of Forensic Science in Corning, New York.

MacDonell set up an experiment. He found space in a high school near his home. On the school stage, he built a stairway just like the one in the Johnson home. He then hired a young model named Heather Murphy to re-create the fall. Murphy was the same height and weight as Janice Johnson.

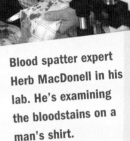

Blood spatter expert Herb MacDonell in his lab. He's examining the bloodstains on a man's shirt.

Murphy strapped on a safety harness. Then she let herself "fall" down the stairs. Dr. MacDonell had marked sections of the stairs with blue chalk. The chalk rubbed off on Murphy's body where she touched the stairs and wall.

This test proved that Norton's theory could be right. A backward fall could have produced the wounds on Janice Johnson's body. MacDonell wrote up a report. "I find nothing that suggests a beating of any kind occurred in the Johnson home," he said.

Lockyer and Campbell decided that they had enough evidence to get Johnson out of jail. In March 1998, they turned over their research to the Canadian minister of justice. They asked that Johnson be given a new trial.

# A SAFE LANDING

## Here's how Herb MacDonell proved that Janice Johnson could have fallen backward.

Herb MacDonell wanted to test Dr. Linda Norton's theory that Janice Johnson could have fallen backward. But how could he do that without hurting someone?

MacDonell got an idea when he read about a local production of the play *Peter Pan*. In the play, actors were hooked up to a safety harness so they could appear to fly over the stage. MacDonell asked one of the actors, Heather Murphy, if she would take part in his test—using a safety harness. Murphy immediately agreed to help. These pictures are from a video of the test.

The stairway was just like the one in the Johnsons' home. And Heather Murphy was the same height and weight as Janice Johnson.

During the test, Murphy was attached to a safety harness. And Herb MacDonell (left) was careful that her head didn't strike the stairs.

Though it's not clear from these photos, MacDonell had marked the stairs with chalk. That way, he could see what parts of Murphy's body struck the stairs.

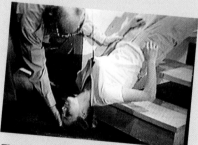

The test proved that Janice Johnson could have fallen backward and had the kind of injuries that were found in the autopsy. (Note the safety harness.)

# Free at Last

**Clayton Johnson is released after more than five years in prison.**

In September 1998, the minister of justice decided to release Clayton Johnson. Johnson walked out of jail after five years behind bars.

Four months later, Canadian officials dug up his wife's body. Dr. Linda Norton flew to Nova Scotia. She and a team of pathologists performed a second autopsy on Janice Johnson. For four days, they worked on the body. They found a **fracture** at the base of the **skull** that was probably produced by a backward fall. "We were able to see that the base of the skull was lifted up about a half an inch," says Norton.

Almost ten years after her death, Janice Johnson's body was dug up for a second autopsy. Experts agreed that the skull fracture could have been caused by a backward fall down the stairs.

By the end of the autopsy, the team members released their findings. Janice Johnson probably died accidentally after falling backward down her basement stairs.

In February 2002, the Canadian government dropped the charges against Johnson. Thirteen years after his wife's death, Clayton Johnson had finally been cleared.

Johnson got a public apology from the Canadian government. He was also awarded more than two million dollars.

Johnson has forensic science to thank for his freedom. Otherwise, says Dr. Norton, he "would still be sitting in jail accused of a crime that did not even occur."

Instead, Clayton Johnson is living near his daughters in Nova Scotia. He spends time with his grandchildren and thinks about his wife often. He still sees some of the jurors who found him guilty. They don't talk about the case at all, he says. 24/7

Clayton Johnson leaves the courthouse with his daughters in September 1998. He had served five years of a life sentence. It had been almost ten years since his wife, Janice, had died.

# FORENSIC DOWNLOAD

**Examine this! Here's even more amazing stuff about forensic pathology.**

## IN THIS SECTION:

- ▶ modern forensics in ANCIENT CHINA;
- ▶ tools of the trade for EXAMINING DEAD BODIES;
- ▶ a quiz to see if you should be DISSECTING CORPSES for a living.

### 1248 Wash It Away

In China, a book explains how to use medical knowledge to solve crimes. The book is called *The Washing Away of Wrongs*. It describes types of wounds. It also tells how to distinguish between natural deaths and murders.

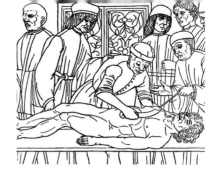

### 1530 Docs in Charge

Emperor Charles V of England orders that a medical doctor must determine the cause of unnatural deaths. Before 1530, coroners—who had no medical background—were in charge of investigating deaths. *Above:* An autopsy in about 1493.

# Key Dates in Forensic

### 1813 Drug Test

Spanish doctor Mathieu Orfila develops the first toxicology tests. He explains that tissue samples should be taken during autopsies. The samples should be tested for poisons. At the time, poisoning was the leading cause of death in murder cases.

### 1915 Twice Dead

New York City hires a medical examiner to investigate deaths. Before 1915, all deaths were investigated by a coroner. The coroner was paid for each body he reported. Investigators found that he took advantage of the system. He left bodies where they would be rediscovered. When a corpse was brought in for the second time, he collected a second fee. *Left:* A morgue in New York City in 1890.

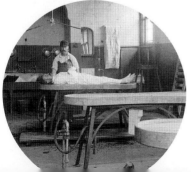

### 1807 Crime-Fighting School

The University of Edinburgh, in Scotland, opens the first forensic science program. The program has a professor of legal medicine.

### Early 1600s
### Early Autopsy

Two Italians, Fortunato Fidelis and Pado Zacchia, begin performing autopsies. They write reports that explain their work. The reports describe bullet and stab wounds. They also describe deaths caused by strangulation. *Right:* An autopsy in about 1666.

# Pathology

**Forensic pathology might be new to you, but it's been around for hundreds of years.**

### 1985
### Gene Pool

Sir Alec Jeffreys develops **DNA** testing. DNA tests help doctors identify victims. They can also prove a suspect's guilt or innocence. Forensic pathologists are now more careful than ever to preserve bodies just the way they are found.

# In the News

## "Dr. Death" Helps Tidal Wave Victims

PHANGNGA PROVINCE, THAILAND—January 13, 2005.

In December 2004, a deadly **tsunami** swept through the Pacific Ocean. The wave hit Thailand hard. It left more than 5,000 people dead.

Each one of these bodies had to be identified. That job fell to Khunying Porntip Rojanasunan. As the *New York Times* reports, she's known in Thailand as Dr. Death. She oversees dozens of autopsies here every day.

Dr. Porntip does not look like a typical Thai doctor. She dyes her spiked hair purplish red. She wears jeans and an ear cuff. She says she chose forensics because she did not fit in as an ordinary doctor. "I work with the dead," she says, "and the dead do not complain."

Dr. Khunying Porntip Rojanasunan is the best-known forensic pathologist in Thailand. She helped identify bodies after a devastating tsunami hit her country in December 2004.

# Autopsy Shows Policeman Died From 9/11 Dust

OCEAN COUNTY, NEW JERSEY—April 12, 2006

James Zadroga spent 470 hours working at the ruins of the World Trade Center after September 11, 2001. Zadroga was a detective with the New York City police. He died in January of **respiratory failure**. (That means he couldn't breathe.)

The Ocean County coroner said today that Zadroga died from dust he breathed in at Ground Zero. A clinical autopsy showed dust in his lungs. It also revealed damage to his liver, heart, and spleen. The report is the first proof that work at the World Trade Center site may have caused **fatal** damage.

**New York City police detective James Zadroga worked for hundreds of hours at the World Trade Center site (*above*). This work may have exposed his body to deadly dust. He died in January 2006. *Left:* James Zadroga's funeral.**

# Autopsy 101

**When there's a suspicious death, pathologists perform a forensic autopsy. Here are some of the steps they take.**

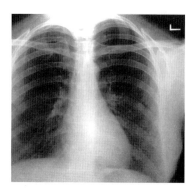

### Documenting the Corpse

All bodies are weighed and measured when they come into the morgue. Usually, they are fingerprinted, too. Most morgues photograph the body both clothed and unclothed. Sometimes, the body is **x-rayed**. The **corpse**'s hair and eye color are noted, as well as scars, tattoos, and other marks.

### Examining the Clothes

The forensic pathologist examines the clothes for any **trace evidence**, such as hairs, fibers, and blood. She also looks for holes on the clothing that could have been caused by weapons.

### Examining the Corpse

The pathologist then carefully removes the clothing. She begins to examine the outside and inside of the victim.

*External:* The pathologist continues to look for trace evidence. For example, she checks for skin under the fingernails. She also notes signs of violence, such as knife and bullet wounds. (See page 10.)

*Internal/Torso:* The pathologist then opens up the corpse's **torso**. That's the part of the body above the waist. She makes a Y-shaped incision, or cut, from shoulder to shoulder. Then she cuts down to the pubic area. That allows her to remove and examine the heart, lungs, and other organs. She also collects samples from the stomach.

48

# TIME OF DEATH

**Forensic pathologists look for three clues that can help them figure out how long a body has been dead.**

**Algor mortis** has to do with body temperature. Body temperature decreases about one degree every hour after a person dies.

**Livor mortis** has to do with the settling of blood in the body. After death, blood cells collect at the lowest point in the body. The position of the cells suggests what position a person was in at death.

**Rigor mortis** has to do with the stiffening of the body after death. About two hours after death, the face muscles become stiff. Twelve hours after death, the entire body becomes rigid. Then the body begins to loosen up. Thirty-six hours after death, the body feels soft again.

*Internal/Brain:* The pathologist then opens the skull. She makes an incision over the top of the head, from ear to ear. She then peels the scalp forward. She uses a saw to cut away part of the skull. She examines the brain in the skull. Then she removes it and examines it more closely.

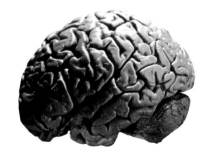

### Returning the Organs

When the pathologist is finished, she returns the organs to the body. She sews up the corpse.

# Autopsy Tool Box

**Have a look at the tools, equipment, forms, and other stuff used by a forensic pathologist.**

TOOLS AND EQUIPMENT

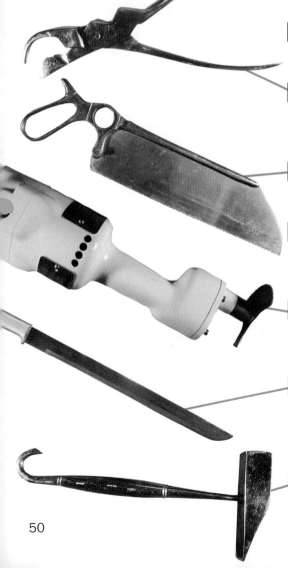

`scalpel` This sharp knife is used to slice open skin and other organs during an autopsy.

`rib cutter` To get to the heart and lungs, a pathologist has to remove the ribs. For that, she uses a rib cutter.

`bone saw` Bone saws are used to cut through human bones.

`skull chisel` This tool is similar to a sculptor's chisel. It's used to separate the skull bone from the brain.

`vibrating saw` The human brain is protected by a thick skull. To cut through it requires a vibrating saw.

`knife` Large knives with rough edges are used to cut slices of organs. Forensic pathologists often examine the slices under a microscope.

`hammer with hook` This tool pulls the skull off the body to reveal the brain.

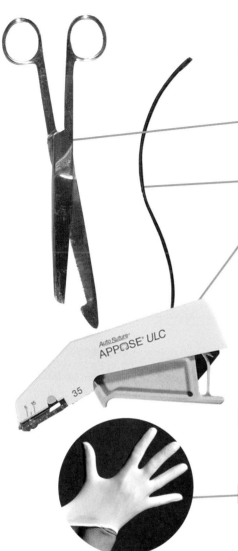

**scissors** Sharp scissors are used to cut through skin, blood vessels, and soft organs.

**enteretome** Pathologists need a special kind of scissors to cut through the intestine.

**hagedorn needle** A hagedorn needle is used to sew up the body after the autopsy.

**staple gun** Sometimes a staple gun is used to close incisions after the autopsy.

**face shield** Forensic pathologists wear face shields to protect their eyes from blood and pieces of bone. This shield also helps to protect doctors from disease.

**scrub suits** Forensic pathologists wear the same uniform as doctors and nurses in the operating room.

**latex gloves** Latex gloves protect the hands during the autopsy.

## BODIES OF EVIDENCE

**Forensic pathologists take careful notes as they perform autopsies.**

Forensic pathologists use these diagrams when writing up an autopsy report. First they note anything they've found on the body—bruises, burns, cuts, etc. A key at the bottom identifies the markings. They also write notes to themselves. Next, they note anything found inside the body. These findings are written up later in the autopsy report.

51

# HELP WANTED:
# Forensic Pathologist

**How would you like to cut into the job of a forensic pathologist? Here's more information about the field.**

## Q&A: DR. LINDA NORTON

**24/7: How did you get started as a forensic pathologist?**

**DR. LINDA NORTON:** Well, I went to medical school. Then I became interested in forensic pathology. I started out at the Chief Medical Examiner's Office in North Carolina. I did most of my training at Duke University. Over 80 percent of what we did were homicides. Then, four months into my training, a DC-9 airplane crashed, so my focus shifted.

**24/7: How do you put all the pieces together when you're trying to figure out the manner and cause of death?**

**NORTON:** One of the lessons I've learned is that you can never have too much information. In fact, my daughters have been my "victims" on many occasions. I once had my oldest daughter lie in the tub in the same position a victim was in when she was found. I wanted to figure out how this young girl drowned.

**24/7:** What would you tell young people interested in forensic pathology?

**NORTON:** We desperately need bright young minds coming into this field. This really is a fascinating field. You get used to the grosser aspects. You become the only one who can make anything out of this kind of evidence.

**24/7:** What kind of training do you need to become a forensic pathologist?

**NORTON:** First, you have to be pre-med in college. Then you need to specialize in pathology for one year. Then you do a five-year residency program. You're 30 when you end up with your first real job. But you can be 30 and have a job that you just love, or a job where you're not as challenged. It's an exciting profession.

**24/7:** What part of your work do you enjoy the most?

**NORTON:** "Putting together the puzzle" is both fascinating and rewarding.

**24/7:** What do you like the least?

**NORTON:** Well, you do carry the odor. It gets into your hair.

## THE STATS

**DAY JOB**
Besides working for states, cities, and counties, forensic pathologists can also work for medical schools, the military, and even the federal government.

**MONEY**
Average yearly salary for a forensic pathologist in the U.S.: $80,000 to $120,000

**EDUCATION**
Forensic pathologists must finish the following.
▶ 4 years of college
▶ 4 years of medical school
▶ 4–5 years in a residency training program in general pathology
▶ 1–2 years in a specialty training program in forensic pathology at a medical examiner's or coroner's office

# DO YOU HAVE WHAT IT TAKES?

**Take this totally unscientific quiz to find out if forensic pathology might be a good career for you.**

**1** **Are you interested in science and anatomy?**
- **a)** I read everything I can about the human body.
- **b)** I think it's sort of interesting.
- **c)** I'm mostly interested in my next meal.

**2** **Are you good at communicating with people?**
- **a)** I'm great at talking with and explaining things to people.
- **b)** Sometimes, but I can be shy, too.
- **c)** No, I get frustrated when I have to explain things all the time.

**3** **Are you curious when you go to the doctor?**
- **a)** Yes, I ask a lot of questions.
- **b)** Sometimes, but the explanations are kind of boring.
- **c)** No, I just want to know how to stay healthy, so I don't have to go back.

**4** **Do you get grossed out easily?**
- **a)** No, in fact I like to watch operations on TV.
- **b)** I don't mind the sight of blood.
- **c)** I feel sick just thinking about that question.

**5** **Are you looking forward to college?**
- **a)** Yes, I've always thought I would get a graduate degree.
- **b)** Yes, but I'm not that crazy about schoolwork.
- **c)** I just want to get a job after high school.

## YOUR SCORE

Give yourself 3 points for every "**a**" you chose. Give yourself 2 points for every "**b**" you chose. Give yourself 1 point for every "**c**" you chose.

If you got **13–15 points**, you'd probably be a good forensic pathologist.
If you got **10–12 points**, you might be a good forensic pathologist.
If you got **5–9 points**, you might want to look at another career!

# HOW TO GET STARTED...NOW!

## It's never too early to start working toward your goals.

### GET AN EDUCATION

▶ Focus on your science classes; take as many as you can. But don't forget English classes. You need to be able to write clear, correct reports.

▶ Start thinking about college. Look for schools with good pre-med programs.

▶ Read the newspaper. Keep up on what's going on in your community.

▶ Read anything you can find about autopsies and forensic pathology. See the books and Web sites in the Resources section on pages 56–58.

▶ Participate in speech-related activities like debate. Forensic pathologists are called on to speak in court and in the media.

▶ Graduate from high school!

### NETWORK!

▶ Find out about forensic groups in your area.

▶ Call your local law enforcement agency. Ask for the public affairs office. Find out if you can interview a forensic pathologist or medical examiner about his or her job.

### GET AN INTERNSHIP

Get an internship with a law enforcement agency or a local lab—in a morgue, if possible.

### LEARN ABOUT OTHER JOBS IN THE FIELD

There are forensic labs in many police departments and sheriff's offices. You can also find out about working in the medical examiner's office. Or try one of these U.S. agencies: Drug Enforcement Administration (DEA); Bureau of Alcohol, Tobacco, Firearms and Explosives (ATF); Federal Bureau of Investigation (FBI); United States Postal Service (USPS); Secret Service (SS); Central Intelligence Agency (CIA); the military forces; the United States Fish and Wildlife Services (FWS).

# Resources

**Looking for more information about forensic pathology? Here are some resources you don't want to miss!**

## PROFESSIONAL ORGANIZATIONS

### American Academy of Forensic Sciences (AAFS)
www.aafs.org
410 North 21st Street
Colorado Springs, CO 80904-2798
**PHONE:** 719-636-1100
**FAX:** 719-636-1993

The AAFS is an organization for forensic scientists. It helps them meet and share information with other forensic experts. Its Web site includes a long list of colleges and universities with forensic science programs.

### National Association of Medical Examiners (NAME)
www.thename.org
430 Pryor Street SW
Atlanta, GA 30312
**PHONE:** 404-730-4781
**FAX:** 404-730-4420
**E-MAIL:** Denise.McNally@thename.org

NAME stands for the National Association of Medical Examiners. It helps medical examiners learn and communicate with one another. The Web site includes recently published research, tutorials, and even job information.

### Armed Forces Institute of Pathology (AFIP)
www.afip.org
6825 16th Street NW
Washington, DC 20306-6000
**PHONE:** 202-782-2100
**E-MAIL:** owner@afip.osd.mil

The AFIP is an agency of the Department of Defense that specializes in pathology consultation, education, and research. This group shares information with people around the world. The Web site has everything from published articles to information about upcoming classes.

# WEB SITES

### Disaster Mortuary Operational Response Team (DMORT)
**www.dmort.org**
The Disaster Mortuary Operational Response Team is an organization that assists local authorities during large disasters. The Web site has information about regional team sites and even online training.

### HBO's Autopsy
**www.hbo.com/autopsy/index.html**
This Web site is from the HBO show *Autopsy*, starring Dr. Michael Baden. It is a terrific resource. The site features real-life cases, videos, a forensic timeline, and an interactive autopsy.

### Miami-Dade Medical Examiner's Office
**www.miamidade.gov/medexam/home.asp**
The Miami-Dade Medical Examiner's Office offers detailed information about how the office works. It's a good site to visit if you want to get a feel for what it's like to work as a forensic pathologist.

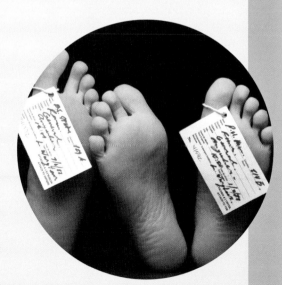

# BOOKS ABOUT FORENSIC PATHOLOGY

Baden, Michael M., MD, with Judith Adler Hennessee. *Unnatural Death: Confessions of a Medical Examiner.* New York: Ballantine Books, 2005.

Baden, Michael M., MD, with Marion Roach. *Dead Reckoning: The New Science of Catching Killers.* New York: Simon & Schuster, 2002.

DiMaio, Vincent J., and Dominick DiMaio. *Forensic Pathology: Practical Aspects of Criminal and Forensic Investigations.* Boca Raton, Fla.: CRC Press, 2001.

Spitz, Dr. Werner U., and Daniel J. Spitz. *Spitz and Fischer's Medicolegal Investigation of Death: Guidelines for the Application of Pathology to Crime Investigation.* Springfield, Ill.: Charles C. Thomas, 2006.


# BOOKS FOR YOUNG ADULTS ABOUT FORENSIC SCIENCE

Innes, Brian. *The Search for Forensic Evidence.* Milwaukee: Gareth Stevens, 2005.

Lane, Brian. *Eyewitness: Crime & Detection.* New York: Dorling Kindersley, 1998.

Platt, Richard. *Forensics.* Boston: Kingfisher, 2005.

Rainis, Kenneth G. *Crime-Solving Science Projects: Forensic Science Experiments.* Berkeley Heights, N.J.: Enslow Publishing, 2000.

Silverstein, Herma. *Threads of Evidence: Using Forensic Science to Solve Crimes.* New York: Henry Holt, 1996.

Walker, Pam, and Elaine Wood. *Crime Scene Investigations: Real-Life Labs for Grades 6–12.* New York: Jossey-Bass, 1998.

# A

**algor mortis** (AL-gor MOR-tus) *noun* the dropping of the body's temperature after death

**autopsy** (AW-top-see) *noun* an internal and external examination of a dead body

# C

**clinical autopsy** (KLIN-uh-kul AW-top-see) *noun* an autopsy done on someone who has died of natural causes

**coroner** (KOR-uh-ner) *noun* a government official appointed to investigate unnatural death; usually not a medical doctor

**corpse** (korps) *noun* a dead body

# D

**death certificate** (deth ser-TIH-fuh-kut) *noun* an official record of someone's death

**DNA** (DEE-en-ay) *noun* a chemical found in almost every cell of your body. It's the blueprint for the way you look and function.

# E

**evidence** (EV-uh-dunss) *noun* materials gathered in an investigation and used to prove someone's guilt or innocence

**exhume** (eg-ZOOM) *verb* to dig up a corpse from a grave

**expert** (EX-purt) *noun* someone who has special knowledge and experience in a given subject. See page 12 for a list of forensic experts.

# F

**fatal** (FAY-tul) *adjective* deadly; having no cure

**forensic autopsy** (fuh-REN-zick AW-top-see) *noun* the examination of a body for evidence in a court case

**forensic pathologist** (fuh-REN-sick path-AHL-uh-just) *noun* a medical examiner; examines bodies in cases of violent, suspicious, or unnatural death

**foul play** (fowl play) *noun* an act of criminal violence

**fracture** (FRAK-shur) *noun* break; something that is broken or ruptured

**Dictionary**

# H

**hemorrhage** (HEM-rij) *noun* a discharge of blood that results from broken blood vessels

**homicide** (HOM-uh-side) *noun* murder; the killing of one human being by another

# J

**jury** (JU-ree) *noun* a group of people who listen to a court case and decide if someone is guilty or innocent

# L

**livor mortis** (LIH-ver MOR-tus) *noun* the settling of blood in the body after death

# M

**ME** (EM-ee) *noun* short for *medical examiner*

**medical examiner** (MED-uh-kul eg-ZAM-uh-nur) *noun* a doctor who directs the examination of bodies in murder cases and other suspicious deaths

**morgue** (morg) *noun* a place where dead bodies are kept. The bodies stay in the morgue until they are released for burial or cremation.

**motive** (MOH-tuv) *noun* a reason for doing something

# P

**pathologist** (path-AHL-uh-just) *noun* a doctor who studies changes in the body's tissues and fluids that lead to disease

# R

**respiratory failure** (RES-puh-ruh-TOR-ee FAYL-yur) *noun* a condition marked by the inability to breathe

**rigor mortis** (RIG-ur MOR-tus) *noun* the stiffening of the body after death

# S

**skull** (skul) *noun* the bony structure that covers the head

**spatter** (SPAH-tur) *noun* the scatter and splash of drops of liquid (like blood)

**suspect** (SUS-pekt) *noun* someone who officials think may have committed a crime

# T

**torso** (TOR-soh) *noun* the part of the body that's above the waist

**toxicology** (tok-sih-KOL-uh-gee) *noun* the study of drugs and poisons in the body

**trace evidence** (trays EV-uh-dunss) *noun* materials like tire tracks, dirt, and fibers that are left at a crime scene

**tsunami** (tsoo-NAH-mee) *noun* a very large, destructive wave caused by an underwater earthquake or volcano

# V

**victim** (VIK-tum) *noun* a person who is injured, killed, or mistreated

# X

**x-ray** (EX-ray) *verb* to photograph with radiation; x-rays help doctors see inside human body parts.

# Index

# Author's Note

**T**here is no such thing as too much research. That's what Dr. Linda Norton told me. "You can never have too much information when you are doing an investigation," she explained.

True, we were talking about the Clayton Johnson case. But I think this applies to other things, too. As I wrote this book I was constantly coming across new information. Once I thought I understood something, I would learn something else that challenged my assumptions and pushed me to dig deeper.

That's the cool thing about research. You keep digging. You read as much as you can. You follow the path wherever it leads you. And you put the puzzle pieces together. I learned a lot writing this book. I hope you've learned a lot reading it—and that it makes you want to know even more.

## ACKNOWLEDGMENTS

**I** would like to thank the following people for taking the time to talk about their work. Without their help, this book would not be possible.

Dr. Robert Middleberg, Director of National Medical Laboratories

Merv Stephens, Senior Crime Laboratory Analyst, Florida Department of Law Enforcement, Tallahassee, Florida

Ray Holbrook, Manatee County Sheriff's Office

Dr. Jan Garavaglia, Chief Medical Examiner for the District Nine (Orange-Osceola) Medical Examiner's Office in Orlando, Florida

Ellen Borakove, Office of the Chief Medical Examiner, New York City

Dr. John Hunsaker, President-elect, National Association of Medical Examiners

Dr. Linda Norton, Forensic Pathologist, Dallas, Texas

Winn Wahrer, Association in Defense of the Wrongly Convicted, Toronto, Ontario, Canada

**CONTENT ADVISER:**

H.W. "Rus" Ruslander, Forensic Supervisor, Palm Beach County (Florida) Medical Examiner's Office

# Contents

# Introduction

## What if?

Ten years of making waves and I'm eager for you to catch the wave! Allow me a quick backtrack: In 1998 I was doing a lot of intricate curved piecing, but was getting bored with the tedious, long process. I wanted to loosen up and make designs that were totally unpredictable and spontaneous.

And that's when it happened. I asked myself the questions "what if I started with a 'feeling' instead of a detailed design? And what if I cut free-form curves with the rotary cutter, pressed the edges under, layered and topstitched them? And what if I continued layering and topstitching fabrics in this manner until I had used all of my pieces?" Wouldn't that be fun? Yes, it is!

In this book, I bring you ten years worth of workshops plus a whole lot of new material on what I call, "Layered Waves." More importantly, here's what to do with them once you have created them.

In the pages that follow, you'll find seven projects with seven different border options, plus a gallery of quilts, wearables, and home accents--to help you steer your own course. My hope is that you mix and match the ideas in this book to suit your fancy.

Feel free to rock the boat! If you find a project that really appeals to you and prefer a different border from another project, go for it! Or, say you love the layered rose blocks, but don't want to be bothered by making a wall hanging. Just make one layered rose block and use it to adorn a vest, or make a few to bloom on a tote bag.

Whatever sparks your creativity will be worthwhile and wonderful. Treat this book as a reference, a guidebook, and a source for inspiration.

Have fun makin' waves!

Karen

# Get Your Feet Wet

## Creating Layered Waves

### Select Your Fabrics

Layered Waves can be made in any color combination, as long as there is a range of values. In the following example, we will imitate the texture, color, and movement of water with printed fabrics that have bubbles, dots, mottled effects, and wavy lines. Avoid busy prints, as they will take attention away from the flowing lines.

6 fat quarters (18" x 22") in the same color family gradated from light to dark

## Supplies

- o   Rotary cutting supplies
- o   Iron and ironing surface
- o   Large and small fabric scissors
- o   Sewing machine
- o   Sewing machine needles: Although we are topstitching, there's no need for topstitch needles. I recommend good, sharp, piecing needles, such as Jeans 70/11, Quilting 75/11, or Sharps
- o   Long pins
- o   Threads: Choose cotton or rayon threads, solid or variegated, to match your fabrics
- o   Tailor's chalk or chalk pencil (optional)
- o   Pin cushion or pin magnet
- o   For needle-turn appliqué motifs: fabric glue and tracing paper
- o   For raw edge appliqué: Paper-backed fusible web

# Layered Waves in 6 Easy Steps

1. **Cut**
2. **Press**
3. **Cut again**
4. **Pin**
5. **Topstitch**
6. **Trim**

## 1. Cut: Rotary-cut a curve

Select one of your fabrics. Place the fabric on the cutting mat.
**If you are right handed**, begin on the right edge of the fabric and cut a curve towards the left edge of the fabric.
**If you are left handed**, begin on the left edge of the fabric and cut a curve towards the right edge of the fabric.

Concave curves (inside curves) are the easiest to make, because their bias edge stretches nicely and creates a nice smooth line when the edge is pressed under. Avoid sharp convex curves (outisde curves); they cannot be pressed easily.

**Warm-Up Exercises**
*If you are shy about cutting into the fabric, here are two ways you can get the feel of the curve without actually cutting it:*
  o    *Draw some practice curves with chalk.*
  o    *Practice cutting with a rotary blade in the "closed position."*

## 2. Press: Smooth the wave

Once your curve has been cut, press the edge approximately ¼" to the wrong side. To do this, lightly pinch the fabric edge with your index finger and thumb. Slide your finger and thumb along the fabric edge, following with the iron in your other hand. It should be a flowing motion.

Steam is very helpful in this process, but if you steam press your edges, use extreme caution and work fast to avoid burning your fingers.

## 3. Cut again: Rotary-cut a second wave

Choose the next fabric—perhaps another value of the same color, to produce a gradual series of waves. Place the pressed edge on top of this second fabric. Cut a second curve that is similar to the first curve, but this time, vary the distance of the second cut between ¾" and 2" away from the first cut. This will give your waves a sense of movement.

## 4. Pin: Temporarily secure the waves

Pin with long pins every 2", perpendicular to the pressed edge. If heads of pins face out you can grab them quickly as you are sewing. You do not want to sew over them! When you are finished pinning, make sure your fabrics lie completely flat on the table. If they don't, re-pin them.

## 5. Topstitch: Waves of thread

Thread the machine with your choice of matching or variegated thread, and use a neutral or matching thread in the bobbin. Topstitch along the pressed edge, approximately 1/8" from the crease, through all layers. It might be helpful to measure with a ruler to find out where 1/8" is on your presser foot, and then keep guiding the fabric along this point. Sew with a slightly larger stitch than you normally use. For example, if you usually sew at 2.5, move your stitch length to 3. You'll want to show off your thread when you make Layered Waves, as your stitching is both functional and decorative. It is not necessary to backstitch when beginning or ending your stitching at this time. Remember to remove pins as you come to them.

## 6. Trim: Get rid of bulk from the back

Turn the topstitched piece over and trim away the bottom fabric approximately ¼" from the topstitched line of sewing. Press well. Keep this trimmed piece—you will use it later on in the sequence.

Continue to layer by repeating steps 1 to 6 until you have a beautiful piece of Layered Waves fabric measuring approximately 18" x 20" with all the curves gently flowing in the same direction.

# Variations

## Add a Ripple

A ripple is a Layered Wave overlapped by two fabrics.

1. Focus on the last, curvy cut you made, both on the Layered Wave fabric in process, and on the remaining piece of this last fabric. Press the edges of both matching curves to the wrong sides.

2. Place a contrasting fabric underneath these two matching curves. Shift the top curve to the right or left and up and down until you see a curvy shape or ripple that pleases you.

3. Pin one side of the ripple with pins perpendicular to the curved edge, and pin the other side with pins parallel to the curved edge. Be sure the heads of these parallel pins are facing toward you as you sew, so that you can easily remove them as you come to them.

   Topstitch 1/8" from the edge. Turn the Layered Wave over and trim excess fabric from the back, and press well.

### Another Ripple

*Here's the approach to use when adding ripples to borders for a dramatic effect. Start with one fabric, cut a wild curve through the center. Press both curved edges ¼" to the wrong side of the fabric. Place these two curves on top of a contrasting fabric. Adjust the curves in and out, up and down until you have created an undulating ripple that pleases you.*

## Add a Crest

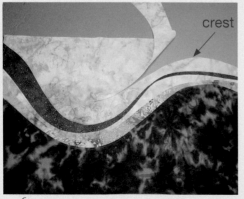

A Crest is a Layered Wave with topstitching along both curved edges. It overlaps the other two fabrics. After creating a ripple, it's easy to create a crest with the next curve you cut.

Cut a curve that varies between ¾" and 2" from the topstitched line. Press ¼" along this curvy cut to the wrong side of the fabric. Place the pressed edge on top of the next fabric in sequence. Pin, topstitch, and trim.

Another approach to creating a crest is to turn your Layered Waves piece upside down, so that the bottom straight edge of the very first piece you started with is now on the top. By cutting a new curve on this straight edge side and topstitching it to the next piece, you will create a crest.

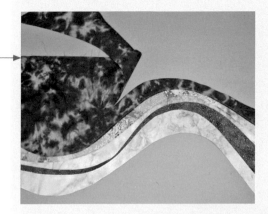

## Disappearing Waves

As you add your leftover trimmed pieces you may notice that they don't quite fit the other curves. When this happens, there will be slender areas where one fabric wave disappears underneath another fabric wave.

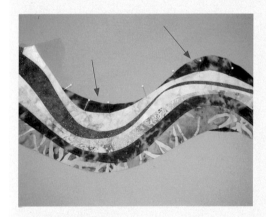

Notice on the sample here how the dark blue fabric is inserted underneath the first section, so that most of the strip is concealed and only two sections are revealed.

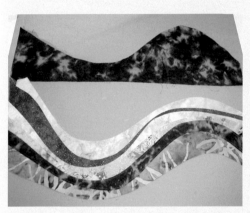

Beginning with a backstitch ½" beyond the intersection of the raw edge and the pressed edge, topstitch the pressed curve. This gives you enough to press under later when that piece is ready to be top-stitched.

Stop ½" before the next intersection of raw and pressed edges, and again secure the topstitching with a backstitch. Then clip the threads close to the fabric surface.

# Rescue Missions

There are no mistakes with Layered Waves! A certain amount of randomness adds to the organic, natural effect. Just the same, there are times when the look is not quite to your satisfaction. No worries! Here's how to navigate troubled waters.

PROBLEM: One of the layers is too wide!

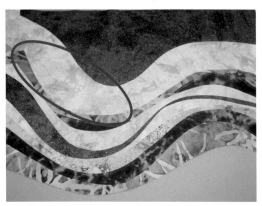

Simply slice a gentle curve through the center of the wide layer, press both edges under, and insert a contrasting fabric to create a ripple.

SOLUTION: Add a ripple!

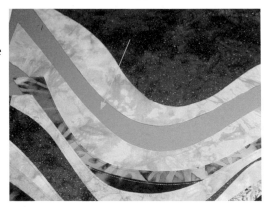

PROBLEM: A gaping hole!

Sometimes holes or gaps can appear in the center of Layered Waves or along the outer edges. Finger-press the raw edges that surround the gap, and insert a scrap of contrasting fabric underneath. Pin and topstitch in place. Trim the back and press well.

SOLUTION: Insert a filler fabric!

PROBLEM: My waves are *too* wavy!

If the edges of your Layered Wave fabric do not lie flat, take out the topstitching from the offending area.

SOLUTION: Re-topstitch to flatten!

With the layers flattened out, pin and re-topstitch in place.

# Hitting Your Peak

Ready to look sharp? Think of the crest of a wave, or the jagged rocks amid rolling hills. Such angled design lines can add a nice counterpoint -- or a great alternative to gentle Layered Waves. They are made in a very similar way. I like to call them Layered Peaks.

**Layered Waves with Points = Layered Peaks!**

You can cut Layered Peaks using the same 6 easy steps for creating Layered Waves. Add this technique to your Layered Waves, or just use them by themselves. Try this "Purple Mountains Majesty," a lofty example that you build from 6 gradated purple fabrics.

1. **Cut:** Use scissors (not a rotary cutter this time!) to cut several uneven angles (90° angles or greater). Marking first with chalk is helpful.

2. **Press:** Before pressing the angles, clip ¼" into the low dips, or inside angles, to aid in pressing the fabric to the wrong side.

3. **Cut again:** Place the pressed, angled strip on top of another fabric. Cut another angled strip similar to the first.

4. **Pin** the two strips together.

5. **Topstitch** with a matching thread 1/8" from the pressed edge. Pivot the needle at each peak as you come to it.

6. **Trim** the excess fabric from the back approximately ¼" from the topstitched line of sewing. Repeat steps 1-6 to create a Layered Peaks fabric.

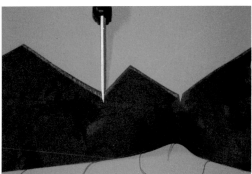

**Congratulations!**
You now know the basics of creating Layered Waves and Layered Peaks. Next, I'll introduce you to some fun projects that will have you working with your textured, topstitched fabric in exciting new ways.

# Smooth Sailing

Time to wade into some fun projects. Don't worry: You'll experience only the gentlest waves and the easiest ways to work with them!

**Shifting Sands**
**(2001)**
*16" x 23"*

# Shifting Sands

For this easy project, you'll create a Layered Waves fabric and then cut your textured fabric into strips. Flipping and re-arranging the strips gives you a fabulous, rhythmic design.

## Fabric Selection

o   6 fat quarters (18" x 22") of tan fabrics in medium and light values that have different visual textures
o   1 yard of contrasting fabric* for Layered Waves, border, and binding
o   ½ yard of fabric of your choice for backing

* Choose any color that you like.

## Cut

1. Cut a fat quarter (18" x 22") from the contrasting fabric. Set aside the rest of this fabric to be used for the border and binding.
2. Lay the 7 fat quarters (6 tans + 1 contrasting fabric) on top of one another so that the horizontal edge is 18" and the vertical edge is 22". Be sure that all right sides are facing up.
3. Rotary-cut a gentle wave approximately 2" from the bottom edge. Press hard so you can cut through all seven layers.

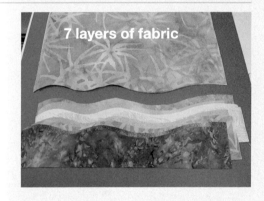

7 layers of fabric

## Press

1. Press the curved edges of each strip ¼" to the wrong side of the fabric.
2. Re-arrange the fabrics by value to create either a gradation or stripe effect (alternating light and dark values). Shift the strips left or right and occasionally introduce a slight slant, in order to create interesting waves. Side edges do not have to be aligned.

## Pin & Topstitch

1. Begin with the bottom two strips*. Place the bottom strip on top of the second strip so that the distance between the top edges varies from 1/8" to 2". Pin perpendicular to the pressed edge, approximately every 2".
2. Topstitch with a thread that matches the fabric.
3. Continue pinning and topstitching the remaining strips

* As an alternative, you may want to pin and topstitch all 7 strips at the same time (not shown in photo).

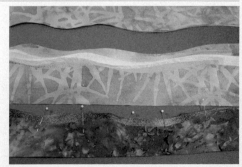

## Trim

1. Turn the piece over and trim excess fabric approximately ¼" from the topstitched line of sewing.

2. Reserve any trimmed-off strip that is at least 2" wide. If it is narrower than that, it is too skinny to be of use.

## Repeat the Process

1. Continue topstitching until all the seven strips have been used. Then take the strips that you have trimmed away from the back and add those into the Layered Waves fabric. Be creative and have fun with the placement of the wave strips.

2. Now go back to the 7 layers of fabric and cut another gentle wave approximately 2"- 3" from the bottom edge, different from the first. Press hard to cut through all seven fabrics.

3. Press one curved edge of each strip ¼" to the wrong side of the fabric and topstitch it to your layered fabric. Continue in this manner until you create a fabric approximately 18" x 22" in size.

## Assembly

1. With the waves running horizontally, use a ruler to rotary-cut vertical strips in the following widths:

> One strip 4½" wide
> Two strips 1½" wide
> Three strips 2½" wide

> **Cut Loose**
> *These directions are merely suggestions. Feel free to cut the strips into a different combination of widths.*

2. Flip some of the strips so that the bottom edge of the strips becomes the top. Remember, these are suggested guidelines. Play with the strips and flip them around to assess the beautiful rhythms they create. Re-arrange, stagger, shift, and flip the strips to produce a design that pleases you.

3. Pin the first two strips together, with right sides facing and long edges even. Stitch, leaving ¼" seam allowances. Continue joining the strips in sequence.

4. Press seam allowances toward the 2nd, 4th and 6th strips. Square the top and bottom, making sure all sides are straight. Your Shifting Sands quilt top should measure approximately 12" x 22".

# Gentle Wave Border

1. Cut two strips: 2″ x width of your Shifting Sands. These will be your top and bottom borders, which will be slightly narrower than the side borders.

2. Press one long edge of each strip ¼″ to the wrong side.

3. Pin the pressed edges to the top and bottom edges of the quilt.

4. Topstitch with matching thread, keeping 1/8″ from the pressed edge.

5. Cut two strips: 3″ x length of your Shifting Sands + top and bottom borders.

6. Press one long edge of each strip ¼″ to the wrong side. Pin the pressed edges to the left and right sides of the quilt. Topstitch with matching thread.

7. Baste, quilt, add binding, and hanging sleeve (see page 94 for Quilt-making Basics).

**It's OK to Piece**
*Borders may need to be pieced or better yet, topstitched together to get the necessary width or length.*

# Quilting Suggestions

Quilt just inside or beyond the topstitched curves to add real texture and dimension to your Shifting Sands. A few lines of quilting in each section that echo the topstitched waves are all that is necessary to complete your piece.

# Variations

Layered Waves in cool blues and greens provide a very different look than the warm sand colors.

There are many ways to arrange and assemble the strips. Move the strips around to audition various looks-- just as in the Shifting Sands project.

**Shifting Currents (2008)**
*32" x 24"*

For the final composition, however, I decided to use the strips quite differently....having each strip turn a corner. You've just got to play with the strips of Layered Waves to discover for yourself the world of possibilities!

Get right to the point by creating a Layered Peaks fabric with lots of angles. Then cut it into 4″ vertical strips and re-arrange them. Add Layered Peaks at the top and bottom.

**Shifting Rocks (1998)**
*23″ x 33″*

15

**Whirlpool (2001)**
30″ x 30″

# Whirlpool

Your waves will be getting a little wilder in this quilt! All you do is create four squares of 12½" Layered Waves. Three squares will be dark and medium blues, and the fourth square will be a gradation of medium to light sea greens and blues. Then, you'll cut all the squares into quarters, re-arrange them, and sew them together to create a swirling effect.

## Fabric Selection

Choose fabrics that look like water. Batiks, dots, bubbles, wavy lines, and striped fabrics work well.

- o  6 half-yard cuts, gradated from dark blue to medium blue*
- o  6 fat quarters (18" x 22"), gradated from medium to very light in sea-greens and/or blues
- o  ¼ yard of light blue for inner border
- o  ¾ yard of dark blue for outer border
- o  1 yard of desired fabric for backing
- o  ¼ yard of medium blue for binding

* Divide your half-yard cuts in half so that you have two fat quarters of each fabric. Fat quarters are a convenient size to work with for this project.

## Cut & Press

1. Starting with the darkest blue value from the dark blue gradation, place a fat quarter on the cutting board.
2. **If you are right-handed,** start at the lower right hand corner and cut a curve with a rotary cutter from the right edge to the bottom edge. **If you are left handed,** start at the lower left corner and cut from the left edge to the bottom edge.
3. Press the cut edge ¼" to the wrong side of the fabric. Place this pressed piece on top of the second fabric in gradated order. Keep the straight side edges of the fabrics aligned.

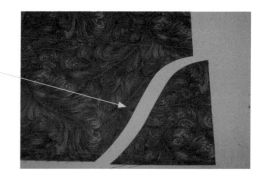

## Cut, Pin, Topstitch, Trim

1. Cut a second curve varying in width from ¾" to no more than 1½" from the first pressed curve.
2. Pin and topstitch 1/8" from the pressed edge.
3. Turn the topstitched piece over and cut away approximately ¼" from the topstitched line of sewing.
4. Save the trimmed piece that has been cut away to be used later in the layering sequence.

1. Press a ¼" to the wrong side of the second fabric in sequence. Place this new unit (first and second fabric) on top of the corner of the third fabric in gradated order. Use the side and bottom edges again as guidelines for placement.

2. Your waves can get pretty wild now. Just remember that the concave curves stretch and press very easily, whereas the convex curves are harder to manipulate.

   Use a ruler or quilter's square to help you visualize the dimensions of the 12½" square.

   Cut a new and exciting curve that varies in width from the second curve about ¾"- 1½" Pin, topstitch and cut away the back fabric.

### Ride the Waves

*You don't have to plan what your square will look like, just relax and let the waves determine what happens! As you begin to use up your fabric, you'll find creative ways to position the scraps so that you get the most use out of them. You don't have to worry about working with the grain of the fabric – go ahead and place your fabric at any angle.*

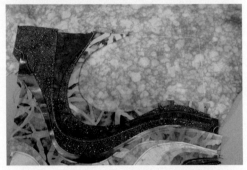

3. As you layer and topstitch, continue to use a ruler or a quilter's square as a guide for the outside edges. Mark the perimeter with chalk. If you do not have a quilter's square, cut a 12½" square out of paper and use that as a guide for the perimeter.

   To soften an extreme curve, insert and topstitch a partial curve. You may want to add a few of these "insert pieces" until the curve becomes more manageable again.

4. When you get to the lightest fabric in your gradated order, work backward towards your darkest fabric. Continue cutting, pressing, topstitching and trimming until you have created a 12½" square. Try to finish the square with a different fabric than the one you started with. Press well after every topstitched seam.

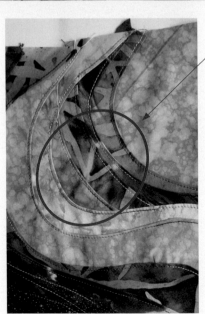

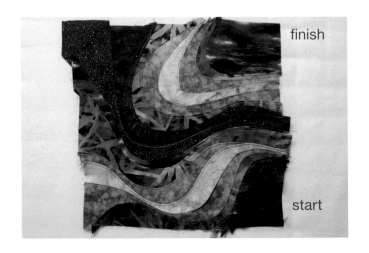

finish

start

6. Make a second square: Begin with your lightest value fabric and end with one of the medium or dark values. Create a wave design that is different from the first square.

7. Create a third square which has a different wave pattern and value placement than the first two. Work from corner to corner, or side to side, or from one corner to a side. Such variations will give interesting undulating lines to the square.

8. Next create one 12½" square using the medium and very light sea-greens and blues shown at the lower left.

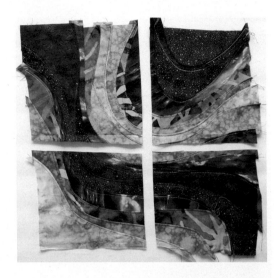

1. Without using a ruler, divide each square into four quarters. If you need a rough guideline for cutting, fold each square into quarters then cut along the fold lines.

2. Place your blocks on a vertical design wall, if available. Working with a 4 x 4 format, arrange the four quarters cut from the medium/ very light sea green square in the center, surrounded by the 12 dark blue fabric quarters.

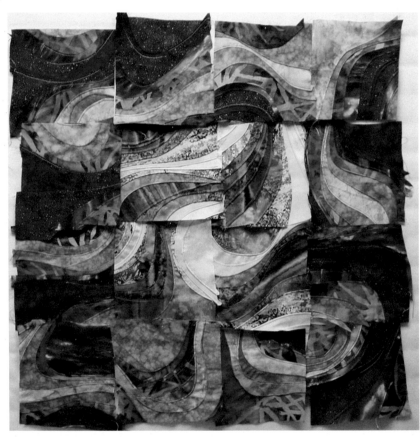

**What a View!**

*Use a reducing glass, or take a digital photo to get a more objective view of your design. I find it very helpful to turn the lights off, because then I can concentrate on the values and the patterns without being distracted by the colors.*

3. Play around with the arrangement. Be sure to flip, rotate, and mix things up. I like to put the squares with the sharpest curves in the four corners to bring the viewer's eye around in a circle.

Your eye will naturally follow the lines of the lightest value. Squint as you look at your design and create a pattern by moving your blocks around.

4. Once you are happy with the arrangement of your blocks, select the top 2 blocks in the left corner of the first row. Cut a gentle curve with a rotary cutter on the right edge of your upper left block. Cut as little from the block as possible, and let the shape of the block tell you what kind of curve to cut.

5. Place the curved edge of the left block on top of the left side of the next block, *with right sides facing up*. Use the curved edge of the left block as a guide to cut a matching edge on the left side of your next block. When the block is repositioned, you can see the matching curves.

   Trim the top edges so they are exactly even. Starting at the top of the block, line up the fabric blocks, with right sides together. Manipulating about an inch in front, gently ease the edges together as you sew, using a ¼" seam allowance. Be careful not to stretch the fabric. Don't worry that the bottom edges are uneven when you reach the end of the seam. It's supposed to look that way.

6. In the same manner, finish sewing the other blocks together in that row, and join the blocks in the other rows. To help keep the rows in order, place one pin in the top left corner block to indicate the first row, two pins in the top left corner block of the second row to indicate the second row, and so on.

7. Press the seam allowances to one side. Join the rows by cutting a gently curved line on the bottom edge of the first row. Use the newly cut bottom edge of the first row as a guide to cut the curve on the top of the second row. The corner points of the squares will not match as they do in traditional patchwork piecing. Our main concern is the waves –the swirling and blending of the colors. Once all the rows have been joined together, press well.

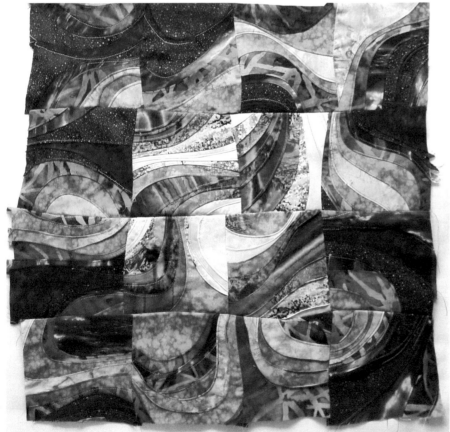

1. Cut four 2″ wide strips selvage to selvage.

2. Trim one of the strips slightly longer than the length of the right side of your Whirlpool.

3. Cut a gentle curve along the right side of the quilt. Use the trimmed edge as a guide to cut a curve along the left edge of the first inner crest border. Press a ¼″ to the wrong side on the curved edge of the inner crest border.

4. Overlapping the quilt top by ¼″, pin the curved inner border edge to the right side of the quilt. Place pins parallel to the edge, making sure you are catching the quilt underneath.

5. Topstitch with a matching thread. Turn the topstitched inner border/quilt top piece over to be sure you have caught ¼″ of the quilt top. Trimming of fabric on the back should not be necessary.

6. Cut a gentle curve along the bottom edge of the quilt top (including the first inner border just added). Cut a border strip slightly longer than the bottom edge of your quilt top plus the first inner border. Use the newly cut bottom edge as a guide to cut an identical curve along one long edge of the second inner border strip. Press the curved border edge, pin, and topstitch to the quilt top.

7. Repeat these steps to attach wavy border strips to the left side and top of the quilt.

## Outer Border

1. Cut four 5″ wide strips selvage to selvage.

2. Cut a very gentle curve on the right edge of the right inner border. Vary the width, but cut no narrower than ½″ from the topstitching. Press ¼″ to the wrong side along this curved edge.

3. Trim a 5″ wide border strip slightly longer than the right side of the quilt. Pin it *under* the pressed edge of the inner border; see photo below.

4. Topstitch the outside edge of the inner border. Turn the piece over and trim away the excess outer border fabric, approximately ¼″ from the line of topstitching. Press. Repeat these steps, working clockwise around the quilt, to add the bottom border, then the left side, and finally the top border. Change thread color when necessary, so it matches the fabric you are topstitching.

5. Baste, quilt, add binding, and hanging sleeve (see page 94 for Quiltmaking Basics).

## Quilting Suggestions

Create a circular flow that connects the blocks. The quilting lines play an important role in churning the waters and adding extra depth to this whirling design. For the best textural dimension, do not cross over the topstitched lines of sewing, simply quilt on either side. Get fancy with your quilting patterns in the border if you like. I quilted swirls to carry the movement of the water into the border.

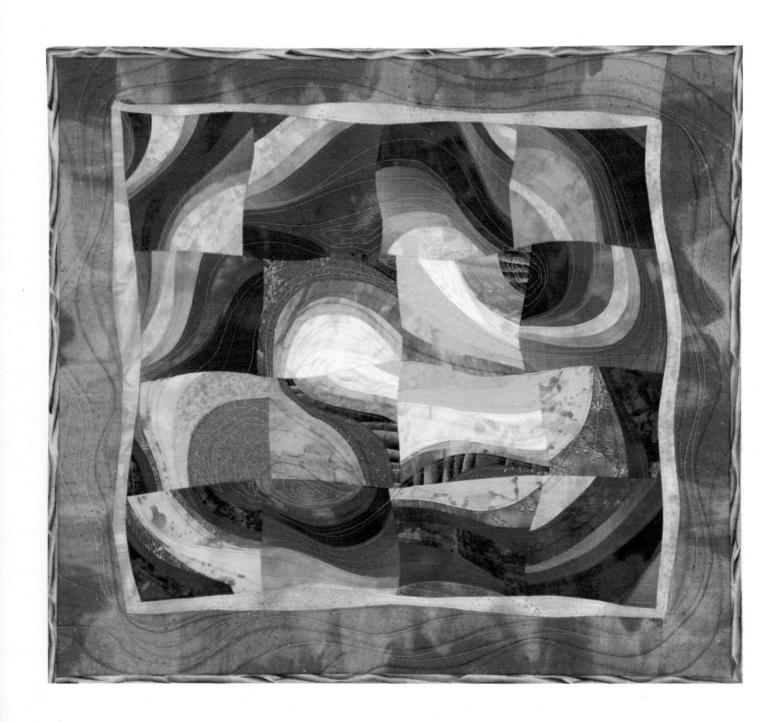

**Salsa & Guacamole (1998)**
*24" x 27"*

Here's an appetizing variation, which uses 3 squares of
hot and spicy reds mixed with 1 square of avocado greens.

**Fresh Cut Fruit quilt top (2000)**
24″ x 27″

A multi-color fruit print combines with bright, juicy colors.
Watch as this quilt top transforms into a market bag. See page 87.

**Driftwood Log Cabin (2008)**
48″ x 48″

# Layered Logs

As you well know, the classic Log Cabin is the most popular pattern in quiltmaking history. Time to build a Log Cabin using wavy logs that look like driftwood from the beach. The charm in applying a new technique to this quilt design is that we don't measure strips, match points, use straight lines, or make the blocks exactly the same size.

We just go with the flow and break out of the box - by allowing the edges to curve and wave!

## Fabric Selection

- o Assorted darks (2" wide strips - minimum length 2"/maximum length 44") of dark grays/browns for blocks
- o Assorted lights (2" wide strips - minimum length 2"/maximum length 44") of light grays/tans for blocks
- o ¼ yard of white for the center of the blocks
- o ½ yard of dark gray for border
- o ½ yard of light tan for border
- o 3 yards of fabric of your choice for backing
- o ½ yard of medium gray/brown for binding

## Cutting the Logs

1. Cut 36 - 2" squares with or without a ruler from the white fabric for the center squares.

2. Select three light fabrics and three dark fabrics. Cut a gently curved 2" strip from each of the six fabrics. The size of your scraps will determine the length of the strips. If you have yardage, cut the 2" strips from selvage to selvage.

3. Press one curved edge on each of the six strips approximately ¼" to the wrong side of the fabric. Some strips may have curves on both long edges, but press only *one* curved edge.

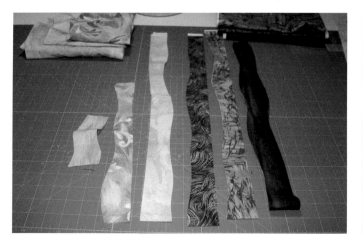

# Assembling the Logs

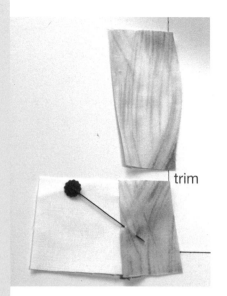

1. Select a light log strip and place the pressed edge on top of the white 2" square by overlapping it approximately ¼". Trim the strip even with the white square. Set aside the trimmed strip to be used in other blocks. Pin and topstitch 1/8" from the pressed edge.

trim

2. Select a second light log (can be the same fabric or a different light fabric). Working counter-clockwise, place the pressed edge of the strip on top of the white 2" square and the first light log overlapping them by approximately ¼". Trim the strip even with the joined unit. Topstitch as before.

3. Rotate the block and continue working counter-clockwise adding two dark logs.

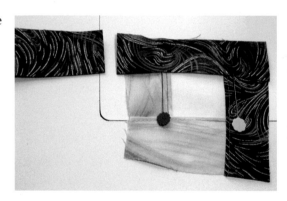

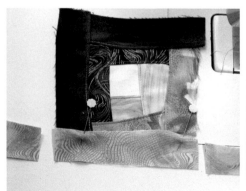

4. Next, add a second pair of light logs and a second pair of dark logs.

5. Continue with the third pair of light logs.

6. Finish the block with the third set of dark logs.

**Size Doesn't Matter**

*The finished size of the block can vary as much as 1½". Aim for a block size approximately 7½"- 8½" and leave the edges curved and irregular. To reduce fabric bulk trim any loose fabrics from the back of the block as necessary. Press well.*

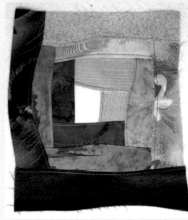

7. After you have made a couple of blocks, you can begin to use the leftover trimmed strips. Start with the shortest strips and work your way to the longest strips. The pile of trimmed strips may get messy, but it adds to the fun of the construction. Make a total of 36 blocks.

Sample Layered Log Blocks

## Assembling the Blocks into Rows

1. Arrange the blocks in the Barn Raising pattern on a vertical design wall. Start in the center by selecting four blocks so that the light halves of the blocks form a center diamond. Continue to repeat the diamond out toward the edges (refer to the finished quilt on page 26).

2. Select two blocks from the top left corner of the first row. Look at the easiest way to join the two blocks. In this case the right edge of the left block has a very nice curve. Press that edge under approximately ¼" to the wrong side of the block.

3. Place the pressed curved edge of the left block on top of the next block overlapping a minimum of ¼". Pin in place, then topstitch. Trim the back.

5. Continue with the next block in the first row. Notice how much larger the third block is in comparison to the second block. Make adjustments for this difference by centering the second block along the side of the larger block.

**Stay in Line**
*Use a horizontal line on the cutting mat to keep the row "straight."*

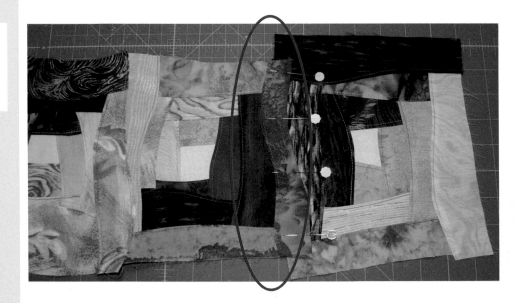

6. Select two blocks from the second row. Mark the top left corner of the first block with two pins to indicate the second row. Assemble the blocks as you did for the first row. Use the first row as a guide to measure how close the blocks should be placed together.

**The Fudge Factor**
*You may have to overlap as much as 1" to align the blocks with the previous row.*

7. Continue assembling the remaining 4 rows in this manner.

# Join Rows

1. Trim the bottom edge of the first row with a gentle curve. The longest and shortest edges will suggest what type of curve to cut. Take as little off as possible; see photo below.

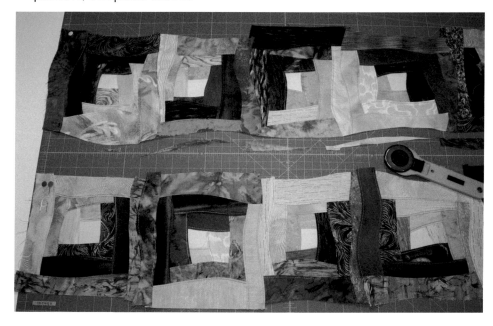

2. Press the bottom edge of the first row approximately ¼″ to the wrong side of the fabric. Pin the first row to the top edge of the second row, overlapping a minimum of ¼″. In some places the rows will overlap as much as 1″.

3. Topstitch 1/8″ from the pressed edge. Trim fabric from the back. Repeat this process to join all rows.

   Your Log Cabin should measure approximately 41″ x 41″. Trim the outer edges to create gentle wavy lines.

**No Borders Option**

*Your Log Cabin can be finished at this point by simply adding a binding. However, due to the curved edges, the binding will need to be cut on the bias of the fabric, to give it extra flexibility to ease around the curves.*

## Layered Log Borders

We will construct the log borders counter-clockwise as we did for the individual Log Cabin blocks, beginning with the first light log.

1. With a ruler and rotary cutter, cut a 6″ strip selvage to selvage from the light tan fabric.

2. Press the right edge of the quilt top approximately ¼″ to the wrong side of the fabric.

3. Place the right edge of the quilt on top of the first light log border, overlapping the border strip a minimum of ¼″. Pin and topstitch. Trim the back and the top edge of the border fabric even with the top curved edge of the quilt top; see photo below.

**Role Reversal**

*To show off the wavy edges of the Log Cabin blocks, the quilt top is being topstitched on top of the borders, instead of topstitching the borders to the quilt top!*

4. With a ruler and rotary cutter, cut a 6″ strip that measures the width of the quilt plus the first border. If you need to piece the border strip, be creative by cutting an interesting curve, pressing it under and topstitching.

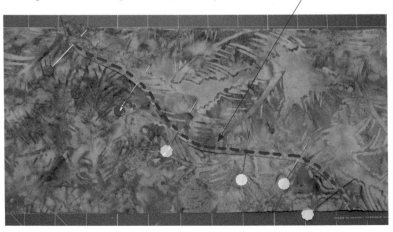

5. Press the top edge of the quilt (including the first light log border) approximately ¼" to the wrong side of the fabric. Place the top edge of the quilt and border on top of the second light log border, overlapping the border a minimum of ¼". Pin in place and topstitch. Trim the back and the left edge of the border fabric to line up with the left side edge of the quilt top.

6. Repeat the process for the left side of the quilt using the dark gray fabric. Piece the fabrics together creatively to get the correct length (see photo on the bottom of page 32). Use a tape measure to make sure the outer edges of the borders are square. Although all of the edges so far have been curved and the quilt top is not an exact square, aim for straight outer edges to frame the composition.

7. Repeat for the last dark gray border, measuring as necessary. Notice the uneven bottom edge of the quilt. On the left bottom edge the quilt top overlaps the bottom border by as much as 3" in order to keep the finished piece square.

8. Baste, quilt, add binding, and hanging sleeve (see page 94 for Quiltmaking Basics).

## Quilting Suggestions

Keep it simple. Quilt in the ditch, or next to the topstitched lines of sewing. Start quilting in the center white square and work counter-clockwise around each block. Parallel lines of quilting in each of the borders are simple and effective.

# Variation

Try this Straight Furrows arrangement with 2″ strips of multi-color scraps. Each Log Cabin block has 24 different light and dark fabrics, raw edge triangles, beads, and star sequins.

Details of
**My Stash at 50**

Raw-edge triangles in contrasting colors are tucked under the topstitched edges, glue-basted, then topstitched at the quilting stage.

Beads in contrasting colors make it fun.

Notice how the beads change in size to match the size of the triangles

**My Stash at 50 (2007) – aka Log Cabin with an Attitude**
(42″ x 50″)

**Random Roses (2008)**
*24" x 24"*

# Random Roses

Here we go round and round to create a beautiful rose. Make just one block to embellish a wearable, or set a dozen-plus-one within wavy lattices, as in this perky wall hanging. Border your floral arrangement with ribbony, topstitched ripples. What gift could ever be such a sweet expression of love?

## Fabric Selection

o ½ yard each of four pinks – one dark, 2 medium, 1 light for the 9 pink roses
o ¼ yard each of four purples – one dark, 2 medium, 1 light for the 4 purple roses
o ½ yard of medium teal for lattice and binding
o ¼ yard of light teal for set-in triangles
o ½ yard each of dark teal and light rose for the ripple border
o ¾ yard of fabric of your choice for backing

## Cut a Rose

1. To make one pink rose: cut one 6½″ square from each of the four pink fabrics. Stack the squares right sides facing up.

   With chalk or a marking pencil, mark 1½″, 3″ and 5½″ increments with a dot on the bottom edge and one side edge of the top fabric square.

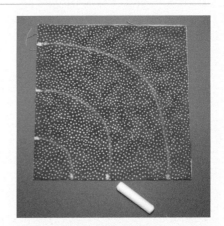

2. Use the dots as guidelines to cut free-form arcs through all four layers.

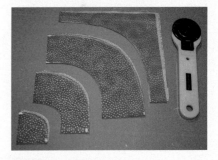

3. Press a ¼″ to the wrong side on the concave curves only (the inner curves) of each of the 12 pieces. The 4 smallest pieces do not need to be pressed.

## Topstitch in a Radiating Sequence

1. Select the darkest of the four small pieces for the center. The other three small pieces can be discarded or set aside for your collection of scraps.

2. Align the pressed curved edge of one of the small arcs on top of the curved raw edge of the dark center piece. Overlap approximately ¼", either pin or hold firmly in place while you topstitch 1/8" from the pressed edge.

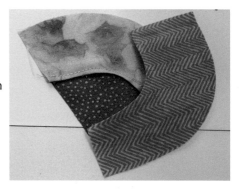

3. Take another small arc and place the pressed curved edge on top of the first unit as shown in this photo.

4. Continue to overlap the arcs, working in a clockwise direction around the center piece, and making sure that each arc covers any raw edges from preceding arcs. The order and positioning of the fabrics is up to you. Mix them up. Aim for contrast and balance. Each one will look like a rose no matter what order you choose.

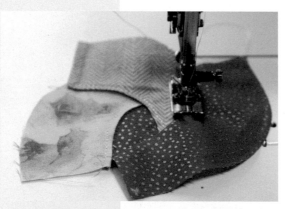

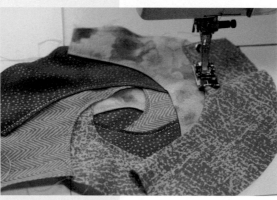

5. As you come to the outside edges, let them be random and uneven in shape. Each rose will be trimmed later to a specific size for this project.

6. Turn the topstitched rose to the back and trim the excess fabric approximately ¼" from the topstitched line of sewing.

7. Make 8 more pink roses and 4 purple roses for a total of 13 roses. Always start with a dark center, and vary the order of the fabrics so that each rose is a unique creation.

## Cutting the Roses and Triangles

1. For this wall hanging project, trim each rose to a 5" square.

2. Cut four 5 3/8" squares from the light teal fabric. Divide each square in half diagonally to create eight set-in triangles for the sides.

3. Cut one 5¾" square from the light teal fabric. Divide the square into quarters diagonally to create the four corner triangles.

4. Arrange the rose squares and triangles in diagonal rows. Join the blocks in diagonal rows by placing right sides together and sewing with a ¼" seam allowance. Press the seams to one side. Then sew the diagonal rows together using a ¼" seam allowance.

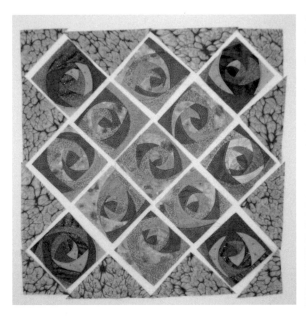

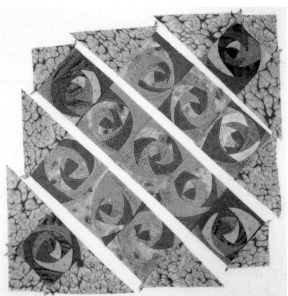

# Adding the Wavy Lattices

1. Cut four gently curved 1½" strips selvage to selvage from the dark aqua fabric. Press *both* edges to the wrong side of the fabric.

2. Cut lengths as needed. Begin with the lattice strips that run in one direction.

3. Pin in place and topstitch with a matching thread 1/8" from the pressed edges on both sides.

**Hold on Tight**

*Pin carefully and sew slowly. Due to the many seams, there will be a bit of bulk to sew through as you topstitch the lattice strips between the rose blocks.*

4. Repeat pinning and topstitching for the second set of lattice strips that crisscross over the first set of diagonal lattice strips.

5. Press well and trim to a 20" square.

# Ripple Borders

1. Cut four 3½" x 34" strips with a ruler from the dark teal fabric.

   Cut four 3½" x 34" strips with a ruler from the light rose fabric.

2. Set aside the light rose strips.

3. Place the four dark teal strips on top of one another, with right sides facing up. Cut a meandering, graceful curve through the center of all four strips at the same time. This creates curves that will be similar on all four borders.

**Variety Is the Spice of Life**
*For ribbony borders that flow differently on each side, cut the border strips one at a time.*

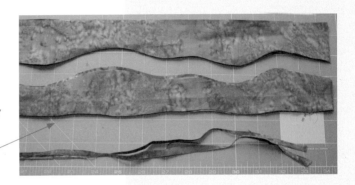

4. In addition, cut a very, very gentle curve on one side only of each of the dark teal strips. This will be the side of the border that gets topstitched to the Random Rose top.

5. Press all curved edges approximately ¼" to the wrong side of the fabric.

6. Place a pair of pressed dark teal strips on top of a single light rose strip, with right sides facing up. Move the dark teal strips left to right, and up to down, to create a rippling line that pleases you. It's OK if the ends of the strips no longer match. The strips are cut extra long to take this into consideration and to create the mitered corners. Pin in place and repeat this process with the remaining pairs of border strips.

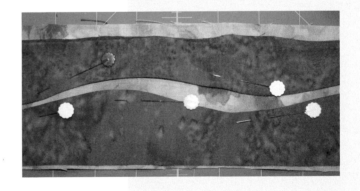

7. Topstitch with matching thread 1/8" from the pressed edges along the two inner curved edges only. Do not topstitch the outer pressed curved edge, this is the edge that will get topstitched to the Random Rose top. Repeat this process for the remaining border strips.

8. After topstitching, turn the strips over and trim the light rose fabric ¼" from the topstitched line of sewing.

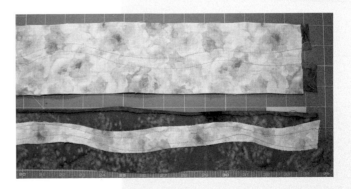

# Mitered Corners the Easy Way

1. Place all the strips around the quilt top with the pressed curved edges overlapping the quilt top by approximately ¼".

2. Select a corner. Fold under the border strip until the pink ripples match. This will not necessarily be a straight 45° angle. It will be whatever angle or curve it takes to match the two pink ripple sections. Move the strips as necessary to create a match. Pin the mitered corner and the border strip to the top of the quilt top.

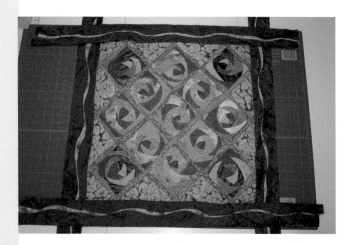

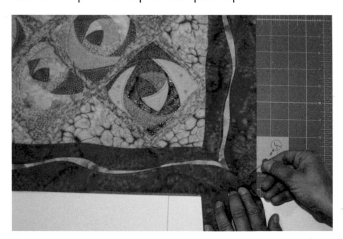

3. Continue to the next corner, pinning the border strip to the quilt top. When you get to the next corner, fold under the border strip to match the two pink ripple sections. Make necessary adjustments to the strips.

4. Continue around the quilt top until all border strips and corners are securely pinned.

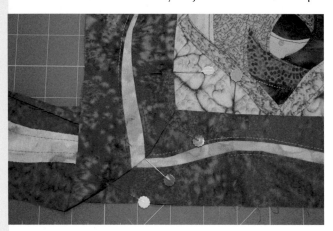

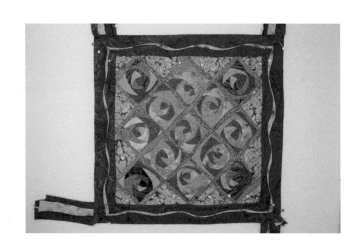

5. Topstitch the border strips onto the quilt top 1/8" from the pressed edges, including the mitered corners.

6. Do not stitch in the pink ripple sections. Stitch that section later with matching thread.

7. Turn the piece over and trim mitered corners ¼" from the topstitched line of sewing. Press well.

8. Baste, quilt, add binding, and hanging sleeve (see page 94 for Quiltmaking Basics).

## Quilting Suggestions

Add delicate texture to your roses by starting with a spiral in the center of the rose and spiraling out toward the outer petals. 2-3 lines of quilting in each petal section will really make your rose bloom.

## Rose Variations

### A Really Random Rose

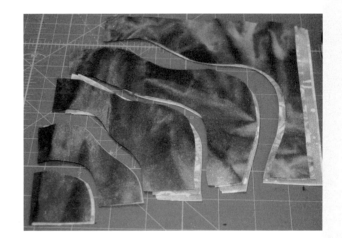

1. Instead of cutting three evenly spaced arcs through the four squares of fabrics, cut four random gentle wavy lines through the four squares.

2. Follow the instructions for the Random Roses project to assemble your Really Random Rose.

### A Single Rose

Rather than a block, consider making a free-standing rose.

Cut it into a rouch circle, angle the edges for a funky contemporary look, or shape the outer petals with scissors to look like a real rose.

Use your choice of appliqué technique to adhere your beautiful rose to a background fabric.

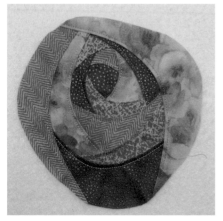
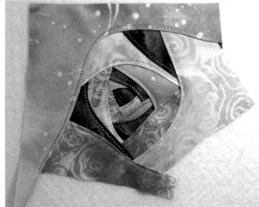

# Variations of the Ripple Border

A ripple border complements any quilt top.
Here it is the finishing touch for a watercolor quilt pieced with 2″ squares.

**Floral Wave (1998)**
35″ x 35″

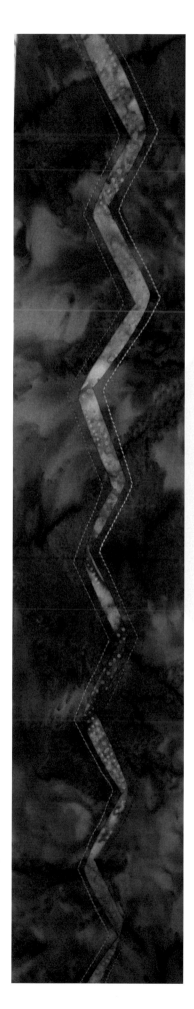

## Zig Zag & Hanging Diamonds Borders

Follow the instructions for "Another Ripple" found on page 6, but cut random angles instead.

Adjust the strips up and down to create a line that zigs and zags; see photo left.

Adjust the strips further apart to create these jaunty hanging diamonds; see photo right.

Contrasting thread for the topstitching adds interest.

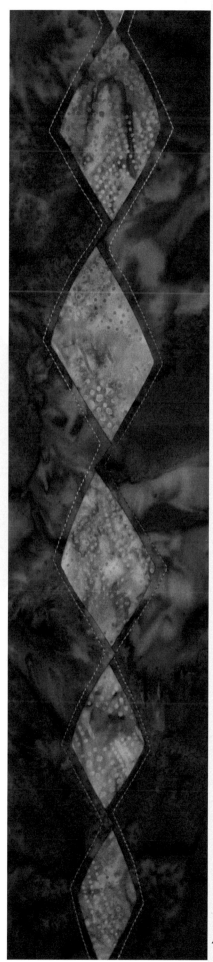

# Surfing the Wild Waves

Warning! Unpredictable currents ahead! These projects with wild topstitched curves will take your creativity to new heights. No more strips or blocks. Now you will create Layered Waves with long, flowing "wavelengths." The end results will be dramatic and unique—it all depends on how you cut the curves. There isn't a wrong way to cut the wavelengths, only "your way!" For these next three projects, I will lead the way and you can follow in my wake. Be brave and see what happens. Are you ready to dive in?

**Mermaid Princess (2008)**
*26" x 24"*

# Hair Waves

What little princess wouldn't love an under-the-sea friend by her bed or bath? For an instant bond, match the mermaid's skin tone and hair color to the recipient's. This little mermaid has a permanent wave! Naturally, her flowing hair is layered and topstitched with wavelengths. A wavy border is the perfect frame, and subtly demonstrates that you're at the "peak" of your quilting skills.

## Fabric Selection

o Four 9" x 18" rectangles of dark and medium reds for the mermaid hair wavelengths*
o 9" square of your choice of color for mermaid skin
o 12" square of scale-like fabric for the mermaid body
o Beads, charms, small seashells to adorn the mermaid
o 24" square of light aqua for the background
o Fabric prints with fish, starfish, coral, etc…to create an underwater garden
o ½ yard each of dark and medium aqua for the borders
o 1 yard of fabric of your choice for the backing
o ¼ yard of medium aqua for the binding

*or your choice of color for the hair. If choosing a lighter color hair, be sure to select a dark background fabric to provide a high contrast for the flowing tresses.

## Hair Wavelengths

1. Begin creating hair wavelengths with the four fabrics chosen for the mermaid's hair, by following the instructions for creating "Layered Waves in 6 Easy Steps" on page 4. Each wavelength will have four fabrics. Make a minimum of four different wavelengths with each wavelength containing the four hair fabrics in a different sequence.

2. After the first hair wavelength has been created, the rest of the wavelengths will be made from the curves trimmed from the back after topstitching. Working with these curved strips takes the decision process out of your hands, since the curves have already been cut for you. Simply pick up two curves and see if you like them together. If yes, press and topstitch. If not, re-cut the curve, then press and topstitch.

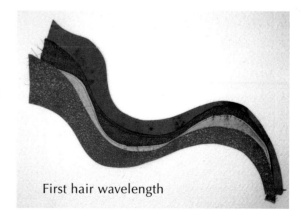

First hair wavelength

3. Keep repeating this process until you have made a minimum of 4 wavelengths. If there are enough fabric pieces left over, create a few smaller wavelengths.

4. Press both outside curved edges of the hair wavelengths ¼" to the wrong side of the fabric. Leave the ends of each wavelength un-pressed.

**A Good Hair Day**

*The key to creating wavelengths to use as hair, is to be sure that one end of the wavelength is narrow and gets wider at the other end.*

**Part in the Middle**

*Create two wavelengths that radiate to the left and two that radiate to the right. This will make hair wavelengths that can be used to flow from both sides of the mermaid's head, unless of course you want all of her hair streaming in one direction. That's fine too. Remember, this is the chapter where there aren't any rules, just suggestions!*

## Mermaid

1. Enlarge the mermaid pattern on the following page 220% at a copy store. The enlarged pattern fits on an 11" x 17" piece of paper.

2. Now you are ready to trace the two sections onto tracing paper: the head/neck/arms section and the body section of the mermaid. The head/neck/arms section extends to the dash so that it can be placed underneath the body section. Place the tracings on top of the chosen fabrics for the skin and body. Pin and cut along the traced lines. If you prefer to use a paper-backed fusible, be sure to reverse the image of the mermaid first. Then follow the instructions on the paper-backed fusible for transferring the image.

**Face to Face**

*If you are using a light-colored fabric for the skin, the background fabric may shadow through. Fuse a second layer of skin fabric to the back to prevent this. Use a fine black fabric marker to trace the mermaid's facial features.*

Enlarge mermaid 220% to fit
on an 11″ x 17″ piece of paper

3. Place the mermaid on the background fabric so that her head is approximately 15″ from the bottom edge of the background fabric and the end of her tail fin is 15″ from the left edge of the background fabric.

4. Select two wavelengths that will frame the mermaid's face. The narrow end of the wavelength should be next to the mermaid's face.

5. Arrange the remaining wavelengths, so that each wavelength covers any raw edges from the preceding wavelength. This process may have to be done several times before you find a pleasing arrangement. Be patient.

6. If a wavelength is perfect for the face area, but hangs off the side, use it anyway.
   Trim the part that extends past the background edge and add it to the other hair wavelengths; see photos below.

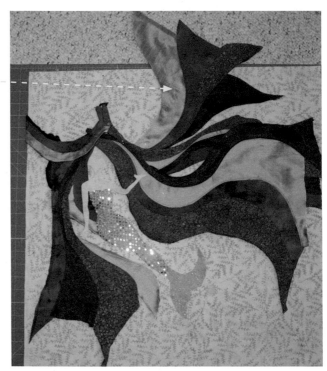

7. To create the top of the mermaid's head, let the narrow ends of the wavelengths come together by creating a nice center or side part for her hair.

8. Trim the ends of the hairwave lengths, leaving an extra ¼" to tuck underneath. Pin.

9. Carefully finger press the raw edges of the hair wavelength under ¼" to the wrong side. This will shape the top of the head. Pin in place.

10. Once you are satisfied with the placement of the mermaid and her gorgeous flowing hair, pin all of the pressed edges to the background fabric to prepare for topstitching.

11. Glue-baste the mermaid to the background fabric. It is not necessary to topstitch her at this time. Save the stitching for the quilting stage. You can also choose to fuse the mermaid to the backing at this time if you are using a paper-backed fusible.

12. Trim the ends of the hair and leave the edges raw. To reduce bulk, you may find it necessary to trim sections of wavelengths that may be underneath another wavelength.

51

## Scalloped Waves Border

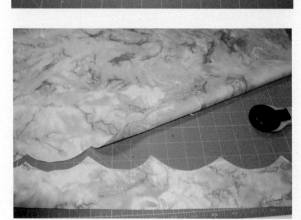

1. Begin with the dark aqua fabric for the inner border. Use the rotary cutter to cut a 4" wide strip (selvage to selvage) with scalloped curves spaced approximately 4" apart.

   ### Cave In
   *For ease of cutting and pressing, be sure to cut and **press only the concave curves** (the curves that "cave in"). The cutting and pressing motion should flow easily in swooping motions.*

2. After cutting the first strip of scallops, let the first cuts be your guide in cutting the next three sets. It's OK that the 2nd, 3rd and 4th strips have scalloped edges on both sides. We will be pressing the concave side only and let the other side be covered by the second scallop border.

3. Follow steps 1 and 2 above to cut scalloped strips from the medium aqua fabric for the outer border.

4. After cutting the first strip of scallops from the medium aqua fabric, the bottom convex curves will need to be trimmed straight with the ruler, because they will become the outside edges of the quilt top; see photo below.

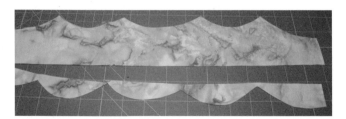

5. Press the concave edges only on all eight strips.

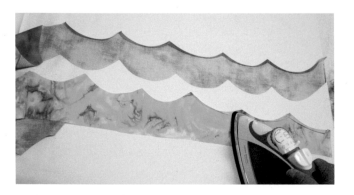

6. Place the four dark aqua borders (right sides facing up) around the perimeter of the quilt top, so that the raw edges of the border strips align with the raw edges of the quilt top. Adjust the strips up and down or side to side to create interesting corners. Your mermaid's hair may flow under or over the border waves.

7. When you like the look, pin all four borders and top-stitch 1/8" from the pressed edge with matching thread.

8. Trim the extra length of the borders from the back.

9. Next, place the four medium aqua borders on top of the dark aqua borders. Adjust the strips up and down or side to side to create a pleasing interaction between the two border strips. Pin all four borders and topstitch 1/8" from the pressed edge with matching thread.

10. Trim the extra length of the borders from the back and also beneath the hair wavelengths if they extend into the borders.

11. Now it's time to create an underwater paradise for your mermaid by adding fish, starfish, seaweed, coral, etc… or whatever will make you and your mermaid happy.

12. Baste, quilt, add binding, and hanging sleeve (see page 94 for Quiltmaking Basics).

## Quilting Suggestions

Outline-stitch the body of the mermaid with matching thread. Follow the lines of the flowing hair by quilting wavy lines in the hair sections. Quilt swirling circles in the background water. Finish the quilting in the border by echo-quilting the scalloped edges.

After the quilting is finished, add small beads for the eyes, charm seashell earrings, tiara, starfish necklace, and other embellishments.

53

**Scalloped Waves Variation**

Stagger the scalloped strips so that the points are centered under the curve of the next strip. Use this variation as a border or as wavy water in a landscape.

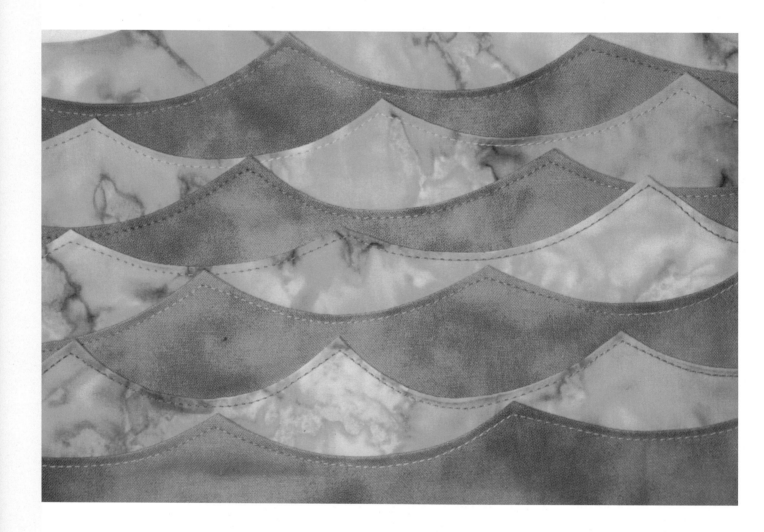

**Mane Ideas**

*How about creating the long flowing hair of Rapunzel? Or picture the flowing mane of a horse as he or she gallops into the wind?*

Wild waves of blond locks frame this mysterious face. My daughter Juli drew the face; I transferred it to fabric and added the hair wavelengths. Gold threads and yarn add some extra bounce and curls to the hair.

**Juli's Hair Waves (2002)**
27" x 30"

**Black-Eyed Susans (2008)**
21½" x 26½"

# Waves of Wildflowers

Here's another chance to loosen up with the rotary cutter and make waves of really wild foliage. In this project, leafy wavelengths become the background fabric for some perky Black-Eyed Susans. An easy, mitered border in a wavy, wood-tone print lets the viewer enjoy the scene from a window...one you can hang on any wall you wish!

## Fabric Selection

o  1 fat quarter each of 3 medium/dark greens for leafy wavelengths background
o  1/8 yard yellow for petals, scraps for brown centers, scraps of light green for buds
o  Thick light green yarn (approximately 3 yards) for stems
o  ½ yard wavy stripe print fabric for border
o  1 yard for backing
o  ¼ yard for binding

## Leafy Wavelengths

Layered Waves usually rely on cutting curves that echo each other. This project involves undulating leaf-like shapes of mirror-image or *opposite* curves. Each of the leafy wavelengths will contain the three selected green fabrics.

Here's how it works.

1. Cut a free-form curve through one of the green fabrics of your choice. Press the curved edge to the wrong side of the fabric and place it on top of another green fabric, with right sides facing up. To create the leafy look, cut a second curve that is an *opposite* curve from the first cut curve. In other words: wherever there is a concave curve (curving in) on the first cut, cut a convex curve (curving out) for the second cut and vice versa.

2. Pin, topstitch, and cut away the back fabric to be used again in the other wavelengths.

3. Repeat steps 1 and 2 with the third green fabric. Cut off the 90°corner, so that no straight edges remain; see photo at right.

4. Continue this process using the curved pieces cut away from the first wavelength.

5. With a few of the left over scraps make little leaves by joining two fabrics. Press one fabric edge under, pin in place on top of the other fabric (see photo at left), and topstitch 1/8″ from the pressed edge. Trim the outer edges to create a leaf-like shape. Then press the outside edges 1/4″ to the wrong side of the fabric.

6. Make a total of six wavelengths using a different combination of the three green fabrics. As you use the smaller trimmed away pieces, the length of the wavelengths will get shorter.

7. If desired, scale down the leafy wavelengths in relation to the Black Eyed Susan flowers by slicing through the center of each of them. Feel free to skip this step and proceed to step #9.

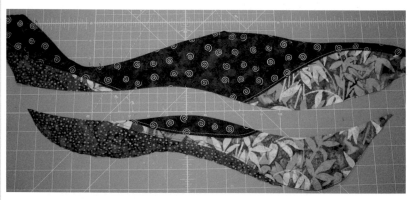

8. Separate the pairs of wavelengths and match them with wavelengths of contrasting value. Press edges under as necessary to join the pairs and pin. The photo at right shows the newly paired wavelengths pinned and ready to be topstitched.

9. Arrange, pin, and topstitch the wavelengths in a vertical format to cover an area approximately 16"W x 20"L.

10. To create sharp points carefully tuck fabric under.

11. With chalk or marking pencil, mark a 16"W x 20"L perimeter. Cut along the chalk lines.

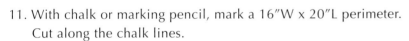

12. Use the cut away pieces and left-over scraps to fill in the holes along the outer edge. Pin and topstitch these pieces. Trim the back.

59

## Black-Eyed Susans

1. Trace the flower images from pages 62 and 63 onto tracing paper or the paper backing of fusible web. The yellow petals and the brown flower centers should be traced separately. If using the paper-backed fusible web option, remember to reverse the images first.

2. Place the traced images on the selected fabrics. If using tracing paper, place it on top of the fabric with the right side of the fabric facing up. Pin in place and cut along the traced lines. If you are using paper-backed fusible web, iron the traced image to the wrong side of the fabric and cut along the traced lines, then remove the paper backing.

3. Arrange the flowers and yarn stems on the leafy background referring to the diagram below. Once the flowers and yarn stems are arranged, baste with a small amount of fabric glue. Adhere any fusible shapes with an iron.

To prevent shadows and bulky lines, carefully cut the yarn stems so that they are *not* behind the flowers; see detail circled above.

1

3

2

+

5

6

Bud 1   Bud 2

## Mitered Corners with a Wavy Stripe Print

1. Cut four 4″ wide selvage to selvage strips with a rotary cutter and ruler. These extra long strips are needed to miter the wavy stripe print borders. Press one long edge of each of the four strips to the wrong side of the fabric.

2. Place the left and right border strips on top of the quilt top by overlapping the pressed edges of the borders ¼″ on the quilt top. In the same manner place the top and bottom borders on top of both the quilt top and the preceding border strips (see page 42 for a similar layout of borders).

3. To miter the corners, fold the border strips under to create an approximate 45° angle. Pin the four mitered corners and border strips to the quilt top.

### Creative Topstitch Mitering
*The angle of the miter does not have to be a straight line at a 45° angle. You may curve or angle this fold to best match a few of the wavy printed lines in the fabric.*

4. Topstitch the mitered corners and border strips. Trim the excess fabric from the back of the four corners.

5. Baste, quilt, add binding, and hanging sleeve (see page 94 for Quilt-making Basics).

**Cheater Curves:**
*To create a very gentle curve without actually cutting it, try ironing a curved edge on the strip by pressing more than a ¼" to the wrong side in a few sections.*

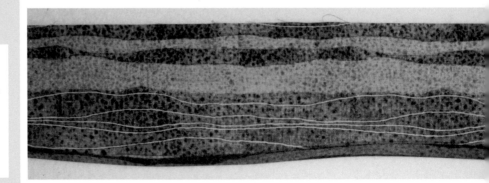

## Quilting Suggestions

With matching thread, outline-stitch the petals and centers of the flowers. Quilt two lines of stitching on both sides of the yarn stems. This holds the yarn in place without flattening it. Echo-quilt the leafy background using a variegated green thread.

# Variations

A leafy background is perfect for any flower, so don't be shy! Pick your favorite flowers and plant them on top with your choice of hand appliqué, machine appliqué, or fusing.

Don't just think flora! Fauna also like to play in the waves. In the example below, a similar Layered Waves background provides a refreshing environment for a happy school of fish. Notice that the waves are oriented horizontally to create water.

Layered Waves for this
water background

**One Fish, Gold Fish**
**(2007)**
*17" x 24"*

65

**Cross Currents (1998)**
30″ x 33½″

# Cross Currents

Steering through these waves can be a real adventure, but just trust your instincts! The course is generally charted, but the final destination will be a surprise! Wild waves crash into each other, giving the appearance of weaving over and under one another. Not to worry, we'll use the same basic steps to make wavelengths that we used to create the mermaid's flowing hair. In fact, the Gallery of Wild Waves is sure to inspire you to head out on your own. Have fun surfing these waves!

## Fabric Selection

6 Fat Quarters* (or fabrics cut to 18" x 22") for wavelengths. Choose a palette of colors that you love in:

- o   One color gradated from light to dark in 6 values
     OR
- o   6 different colors
     OR
- o   1 multi-color print + 5 coordinating fabrics

- *   For larger projects, buy a ½ yard of 6 different fabrics. Divide the ½ yard cuts in half to create two sets of fat quarters (18" x 22") or a size that fits easily on your cutting mat. Odd shaped scraps are fine, too.

## Crisscrossing Wavelengths - The Basic Steps

1. Begin creating wavelengths with the six selected fabrics by following the instructions for creating Layered Waves in 6 Easy Steps on page 4. Each wavelength will have six fabrics. Make a minimum of 6 different wavelengths with each wavelength containing the six fabrics in a different sequence. Wild curves such as "S" and "C" shapes work best.

2. Now you are ready to perform magic. To give the illusion of wavelengths weaving over and under each other, select two of your wavelengths that have contrasting values at the edges. Lay one on top of the other so that they crisscross at some point.

3. Finger-press or use an iron to press *one* edge of the top wavelength approximately ¼" to the wrong side.

4. Pin this one pressed side of the wavelength on top of where it overlaps the wavelength underneath.

5. Topstitch the pinned section only (yellow dotted lines in photo). Secure the end stitching with one backstitch.

cut-off
section

6. After topstitching, trim the excess fabric from the back, ¼" from the topstitched line of sewing. The underneath wavelength (the cut-off section) can now be released and repositioned under the the top wavelength.

If we were to topstitch both sides of the top wavelength, the underlying wavelength (cut-off section) would be shortened considerably at the trimming stage. *Topstitching on just one side* gives us a larger wavelength to play with. It also adds to the serendipity of the outcome – totally unpredictable!

7. Finger-press the edge of the other side of the top wavelength (see circled area).

Place the pressed edge on top of the cut-off section, overlapping approximately ¼". This creates the illusion that one piece flows under the other.

Pin in place.

Topstitch only where the pins are securing the two wavelengths. Press well.

8. Add a third wavelength so that it nestles into a curve, weaves under, and/or covers raw edges of another wavelength. You can even create a hole as seen in the photo, which can be filled later with either another wavelength or background fabric. Press well after each new wavelength is topstitched.

9. Continue to assemble the wavelengths. Reposition any useable wavelengths or make new ones from the scraps. If you notice that your piece is not laying flat and/or is beginning to ripple along the sides, a remedy can be found for this unwanted wave in the Rescue Missions section on pages 8.

**The More the Merrier**
*Each wavelength can have a minimum of 6 fabrics or as many as 12 fabrics. It's up to you.*

## Create a Flow

Once you have assembled several of your wavelengths, step back and look at the flow of your piece. Do your eyes follow the lines easily? Check it out from different angles. Take a digital photo, use a reducing glass or look through binoculars from the wrong end. These different perspectives will amaze you.

Although design walls are ideal for viewing and assessing compositions, these wavelengths are too cumbersome to work with vertically and are much easier to manage on a flat horizontal surface, table or floor.

On many occassions a certain image will appear or you will notice a flowing pattern that wasn't apparent before. A few of the images that have appeared in the workshops over the years have been, fish, birds, underwater gardens, flowers, sailboats, carnival masks, faces, and landscapes.

## Design Decisions

At one point in the design process you need to decide on the size and shape for your creation. Is it going to be a square, a rectangle, a circle, or will it have irregular edges? Will it be used as a king size bed quilt, displayed as a wallhanging, or worn as a jacket? Begin to imagine the perimeter of your quilt and topstitch fabrics underneath and on top of your piece to create the size you are aiming for. Use your scraps to fill in the holes and save larger pieces of fabric to create long flowing waves for your borders.

Let the size and shape of your scraps decide on the placement. Try to react to what's in front of you. Work with only one piece at a time so you won't become overwhelmed.

## Curvy Edges

Curvy edges are impressive and yet quite easy to do. They simply require that you cut your binding strips on a 45° angle across the grain of the fabric. This creates a bias binding that manipulates easily around gently curved edges.

Another way to create a curvy edge is to satin-stitch or zig zag stitch the edges with a matching thread (see the bottom edge of Positive Energy 4 on page 76).

In the next pages I'll show you the design process behind several quilts that use the Cross Currents style of criss-crossing wavelengths.

Every quilt you make using this process will be a one-of-a-kind creation.

**Sand and Sea (2004)** 41" x 47"

The beach offers endless inspiration. Wavelengths of blues for water and tans for the sand intermingle playfully in this quilt.

The process begins with the selection of the first two wavelengths.

**Color Waves (2001)**
42½″ x 54″

Try to work with wavelengths cut selvage to selvage. They are not easy to fit on the cutting mat, but the effort certainly pays off.

This first arrangement of wavelengths looks like a cascading waterfall.

The second arrangement of wavelengths forms a grid. Placing yardsticks around the perimeter helps visualize the final size and shape.

A black background fabric emphasizes the bright colors and creates wonderful negative spaces

## Couched Yarn

As the wavelengths narrow to a point, couch yarns to extend the lines and cover the raw edges. To couch yarns, use a small amount of fabric glue to hold the yarn in place. Then use matching thread to quilt through the yarn with a meandering line of stitching or a zig zag stitch to hold it in place.

**Positive Energy 3 (2004)**  35″ x 46″

This is the first quilt I made when we moved to our dream home in Connecticut. I couldn't contain my excitement, so I let it spill out in wonderful waves of positive energy over this quilt —even into the borders!

**Look Sharp!**

*Add angles to some of your wavelengths—triangular, like prairie points or mountain ranges, and squared off, like crenellated castle towers and machine gears. The eye will immediately be drawn to them. Choose high-contrast fabrics to really emphasize the contrasts of curvy and angular.*

**Positive Energy 4 (2007)** 33″ x 43″

August is a special month full of warm summer sunshine and also my birthday! What a great reason to celebrate by making a giant sun with radiating wavelengths.

A touch of blue for the sky is included in each of the yellow wavelengths. The final composition is topstitched to a red background fabric, which fills in the negative spaces.

This abstract sun begins with the circle of blue. Then three wavelengths are placed around it.

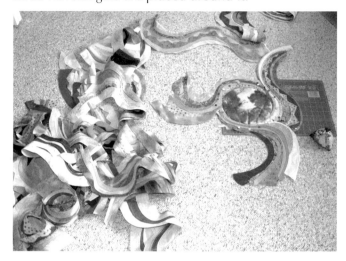 

**Secret Spring (2004)**
*29" x 35"*

Instead of wavelengths of wild curves, here we have strips of Layered Peaks assembled in the same Cross Currents style. Rocks symbolize stability, strength, and dependability. I started with this idea and let the piece evolve.

At one point the lower right corner began looking like a cave with a little waterfall.

I followed in that direction and added water in the form of couched yarns (see "Couched Yarn" on page 73). That final touch became a focal point, and inspired the title of the quilt.

This piece was created as an emotional response to the attacks on September 11, 2001. The overwhelming display of flags during the aftermath was a positive reaction I wanted to commemorate.

What are the colors of your country's flag, or that of your ancestors? How about using those colors as your palette for creating wavelengths?

**Old Glory Waves Again (October 2001)**
*26" x 23½"*

Silver and gold paper star stickers float on the surface of this waving flag. A fine sparkly netting and quilting stitches hold the stars in place.

80

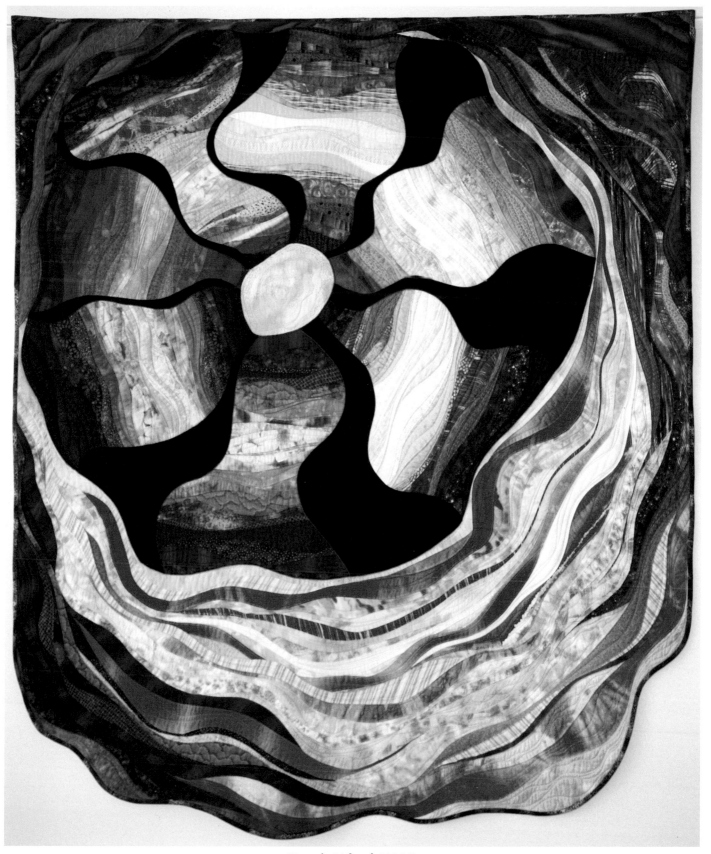

**Cosmic Wheel (1998)**
57″ x 67″

Wavy black spokes connect seven Layered Waves fabrics (not crisscrossing wavelengths in this case) to form the center. Then one wave at a time, the wheel expands and radiates out to the curvy edges.

# Flowing Wearables & Home Accents

Let's dive into our dramatic textured Layered Waves fabrics and wrap them around us in our clothing. With a little inspiration, you'll soon be incorporating your luscious fabrics into your favorite wearables patterns. Patterns for the vest, the basic apron, and the broad-brimmed hat are available from the designers; see Resources. But for most of the items in this chapter, you don't even need a pattern. You'll simply build off of staples that are already in your closet or home, such as a sweatshirt, denim shirt, canvas tote bag, pillow, or journal.

82

**Think Big**
*Use a sweatshirt one or even two sizes larger. This will allow for shrinkage during the quilting and re-assembly process. A larger sweatshirt will also give you the length needed to make a hip length jacket.*

# Karen's Jacket

I recently made this jacket and would you believe this is the first jacket I've ever made? It is, and I want to make more! I didn't have a pattern, just a sweatshirt. I used the fuzzy side as the foundation base and batting substitute for the Layered Waves. The smooth outside of the sweatshirt then becomes the "lining."

The first step is to cut the sweatshirt (or undo the stitched seams) along the sides, sleeves, shoulders and down the front center. This creates flat template pieces, which become guides to creating Layered Waves fabrics in the appropriate size. It's up to you whether you save the ribbing around the cuffs and waist. This jacket has the waist ribbing cut off to create a shorter jacket that comes just below my waist.

Once the Layered Waves fabrics have been created, pin them to the corresponding sweatshirt templates (2 front panels, 2 sleeves and back panel). Quilt as desired. The quilting stitches hold the Layered Waves fabric to the sweatshirt. Now it's time to sew the sweatshirt back together and you are ready to model your new creation.

Layered Peaks add visual impact when nestled among the gentle curves.

# Denim Shirt Jacket

What a novel idea: My friend Trish Palmer decided to use a light weight denim shirt as a base for a jacket. She cut the shirt apart to create her patterns and constructed her jacket using an exquisite selection of batik fabrics.

Below are some of the wavelengths Trish made to use in her jacket.

# Wave Vest

As a student in my Layered Waves workshop many years ago, Trish Palmer made a beautiful piece of textured fabric but didn't know what to do with it. Later, it occurred to her that it would make a beautiful vest panel using Eileen Chapman's "Just the Vest" pattern (see Resources, page 96).

**Flatter Yourself**

*Perhaps you already have a favorite jacket or vest pattern. Use it with Layered Waves and Peaks fabric for a perfect fit.*

Trish used leftover scraps to create the other front panel and added a multi-color print fabric for the back.

# Market Bags

Do you have a collection of canvas tote bags from conventions and festivals that you have attended? How about giving them a new look?

Simply slice the bag up both sides, so that you have a flat rectangular piece of canvas. Create a Layered Waves fabric. Then pin it to the canvas bag. Secure the creative fabric with a few extra lines of topstitching. Sew the side seams back together again. Now you have a sturdy bag that will be the envy of everyone at the farmer's market or the supermarket. It's that easy!

A yummy selection of fruit and vegetable fabrics is a treat to slice.

This design is a take-off on my Accidental Landscape™ pattern entitled "Beaches." The Layered Wave strips for this bag are enlarged and topstitched one at a time.

Once I had the two-sided scene topstitched, I pinned it to the canvas bag and added a few lines of stitching to attach it to the bag. Dimensional waves of lace add movement to this scene.

I knew that it would be a long time before I ever quilted this quilt top, so I made it into a bag. Now it's finished and I love it!

# Yummy Apron

Let's whip up some vegetable wavelengths and mix them together for a tasty combination. My Tossed Salad apron is a take-off on a holiday apron pattern by The Country Quilter in Somers, NY (see Resources, page 96).

A vegetable print fabric combined with three values of green make up the wavelengths for this robust-looking, butcher-style apron. While you are chopping vegetable fabrics, cut an additional piece of fabric in the shape of the apron pattern to use as a lining.

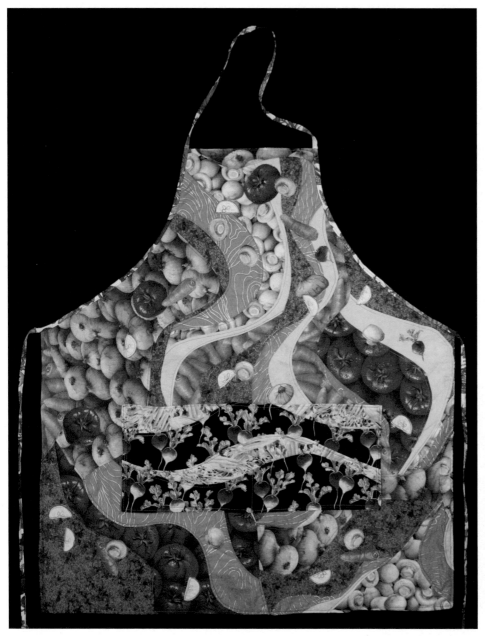

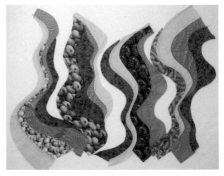

Once the wavelengths are assembled to fit the basic shape of the apron pattern, fussy-cut vegetables from a vegetable print fabric and toss them in among the salad greens using raw edge appliqué.

88

# Summer Hat

Protect yourself from the summer sun with a floppy brimmed hat made with Layered Waves. Fiber artist and designer, Lisa Cruse inspired this cool hat with her Garden Hat pattern (see Resources, page 96).

I decided to add a gradation of six batik greens in flowing wavy lines.

The brim and the rise of the hat are made with Layered Waves fabrics; the crown and lining are cut from pieces of batik.

Torn fabric flowers with ribbon leaves, made and designed by Lisa Cruse, add whimsical finishing touches to this garden hat. Silk flowers from your craft stash or local craft store would be an easy alternative.

# Journal Covers

Get your creative juices flowing every time you open your own, personalized journal. Artist and friend Cat Allard made two journal covers with her Layered Waves fabric, one is unadorned, yet dramatic in its peaceful simplicity. I see an Accidental Landscape, do you? The second journal is embellished with charms, fabric ribbons, and a convenient pocket with pencils that complement the color scheme!

**The Cover Formula:**

*(width + width + spine + flaps) x (height + seam allowance) = cover size for front and lining*

Instructions for the journal on left, a 7" x 9" journal with a 1" spine:

Cut a Layered Waves fabric and a plain piece of lining fabric 20" x 10"
(7" width + 7" width + 1" spine + 2½" front flap + 2½" back flap)  x (9" height + 1" seam)

1. With right sides together sew the two 20" x 10" rectangles with a ½" seam along the top and bottom edges. Leave the ends open.
2. Press ¼" to the wrong side of the two 10" ends.
3. Turn the tube inside out so that right sides of the fabrics are now facing out. Stitch along the two 10" pressed ends, continuing to leave the tube open. This is where the book's front and back covers are inserted. Very impressive, yet quick and easy!

90

# Pillow

Looking for just the right accent for your living room? This quick project is the answer. Make a pillow with Layered Waves and Peaks to coordinate with your home's décor.

This 20" square pillow is made using two 18½" x 18½" squares, one of a Layered Waves fabric, the other of a solid backing fabric. With right sides together, sew the Layered Waves and backing fabrics together using a ¼" seam. Leave a 14" opening on one side to allow for the insertion of the pillow form. After stitching, turn inside out and insert the pillow form. It will be a very snug fit. Hand-stitch the opening together.

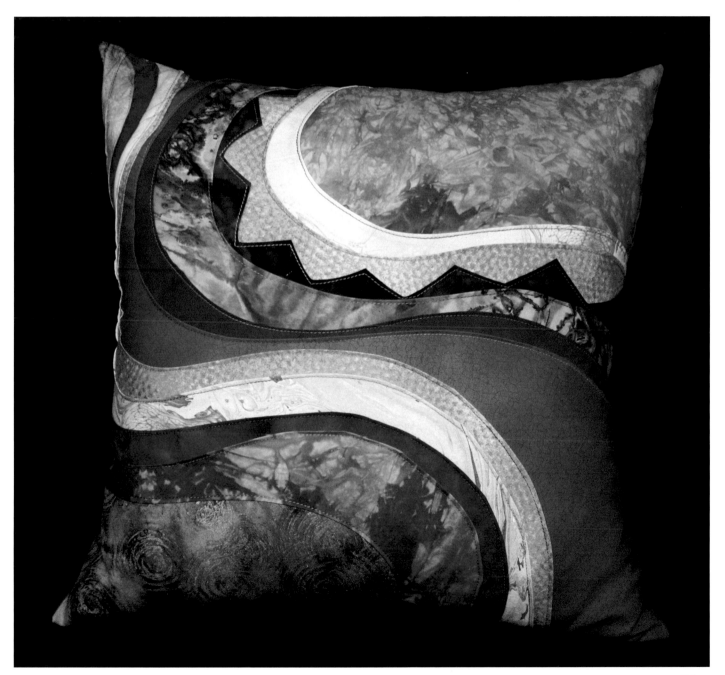

# Matted and Framed

In a time crunch? For a quick gift that requires neither quilting nor binding, just set your Layered Waves fabric under a pre-cut mat in a standard-size frame. Voila! Your gift is ready to present.

This is also a great way to use leftovers from larger projects!

**Shifting Sands 1 (1999)**
within an 8″ x 10″ mat/frame

**Wave 2 (1999)**
within an 8″ x 10″ mat/frame

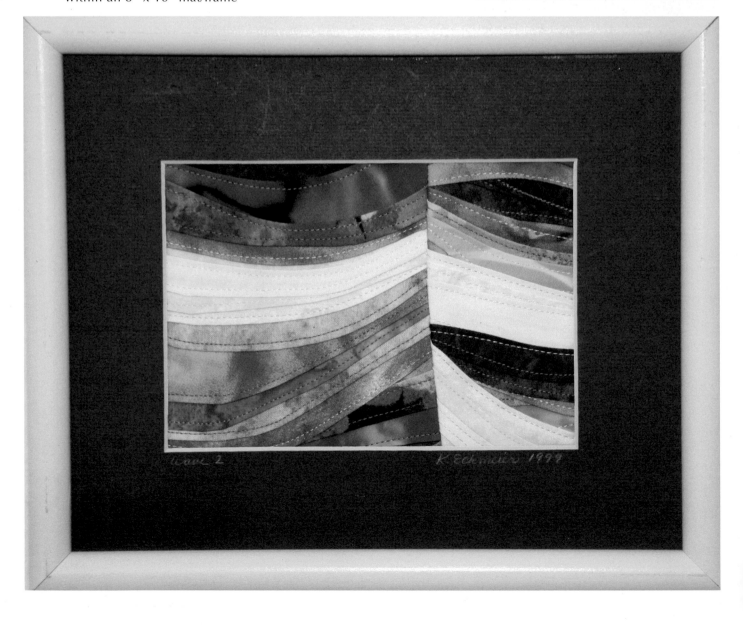

# Soft Frame

To celebrate the special places, occasions and people in your life, try this fun fabric frame. Here I framed a photo (transferred to fabric) of my grandson Rowen on his first birthday.

Select fabrics to coordinate with the colors in the photo. Then make borders with four matching sets of Layered Waves fabrics measuring approximately 5″ x 22″. Keep the curves very gentle so that they do not distract from the photo.

Place the borders around the photo and topstitch-miter the corners. For detailed instructions on how to topstitch mitered corners, see pages 42 and 64.

**Rowen's First Birthday:**
**August 11, 2008**
14″ x 17″
with a 6″ x 9″ photo
transferred to fabric

93

# Quiltmaking Basics

## Basting

o Once your quilt top is complete, square up the edges so they are even and the corners form a 90° angle.

o Cut a piece of batting and a backing fabric approximately 2″ larger all around the quilt top.

o Place the backing fabric right side down on a flat surface.

o Secure the edges with masking tape, so that the fabric doesn't wrinkle.

o Next, place the batting on top of the backing fabric.

o Smooth the batting gently to create a flat surface.

o Place the quilt top on top of the batting with the right side facing up.

o Baste with thread through all three layers in a 4″ grid.

o For small quilts, pin basting is a quick option.

**Flat or Fluffy?**
*For wallhangings, use 100% cotton batting. For functional bed and lap quilts there is a wide selection of batting on the market that ranges from high loft polyester, to warm wool, to light organic bamboo. Choose what best suits the climate where the quilt will be used.*

## Quilting

o Layered Waves projects can be hand or machine quilted.

o Quilting stitches hold the three layers of a quilt together; quilt top, batting and backing.

o Select your choice of cotton, rayon, invisible, or metallic threads to complete your piece.

o After quilting your piece, steam press from the back in an up and down motion.

o Square and trim the edges so that the quilt top, batting and backing are even.

o You are now ready to add a hanging sleeve (only for wall quilts) and binding.

## Hanging Sleeve for a Wallhanging

If your quilt is going to be displayed on a wall for everyone to admire, it will need a hanging sleeve.

1. Cut a 10″ length of fabric. The width will be determined by the width of the quilt. The "width minus 2 inches," is the correct size for the hanging sleeve.

2. On each width end, press ¼″ to the wrong side, then press ¼″ one more time.

3. Machine-stitch a straight line down the two pressed ends to hold them place.

4. Press wrong sides together to create a 5″ hanging sleeve. If you plan to exhibit your piece in juried shows, this sleeve finishes to 4½″ after sewing and will meet the required sleeve minimum for most shows. Shows can vary in their requirements so be sure to double check the prospectus.

5. Pin the hanging sleeve to the backside of the quilt by aligning the raw edges of the sleeve with the top raw edges of the quilt. Center the hanging sleeve so that there is approximately a 1″ space on either side. These two spaces on either side of the hanging sleeve hide the hardware when displaying your quilt.

## Binding

1. Cut 2½″ x 44″ (selvage width) strips that will extend around the perimeter of the quilt.

2. Join the two strips together with a straight or 45° angled seam.

3. On one end only press ¼″ to the wrong side (this will be your starting point), then press the strips in half lengthwise, wrong sides together.

4. Pin to the top right side of the quilt top, by aligning the raw edges.

5. As you come to a corner, flip the fabric strip up at a 45° angle, then fold it down again and continue pinning.

6. To finish pinning the binding, insert the tail end into the starting point.

7. Machine-stitch the binding with a ¼″ seam allowance. As you approach the corners, stop ¼″ from the edge, lift the presser foot up, flip the mitered fabric flap to one side, pivot the quilt top to begin sewing in the new direction, put the presser foot down at the edge of the fabric and continue sewing. Repeat for all corners.

8. Fold the binding around to the backside of the quilt and hand-stitch to the back, so that the line of machine stitching is covered. Miter the corners as you come to them. Hand-stitch the bottom edge of the hanging sleeve.

# Resources

**Hat**
Lisa Cruse
www.lisacruse.com
**Specialty Charms**
Cat Allard
www.zencatart.com

**Apron**
The Country Quilter
344 Route 100
Somers, NY 10589
888-277-7780
www.countryquilter.com

**Vest**
Eileen Chapman: Eileen's Design Studio
4503 Bacon School Road
St. Joseph, MI 49085
888-240-6002
www.QuiltBooksUSA.com

## Check out Karen's other books!

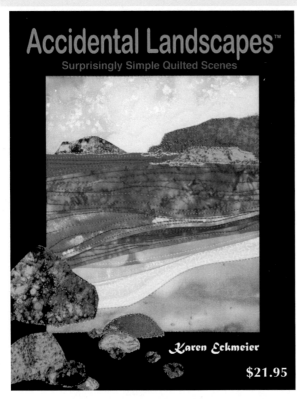

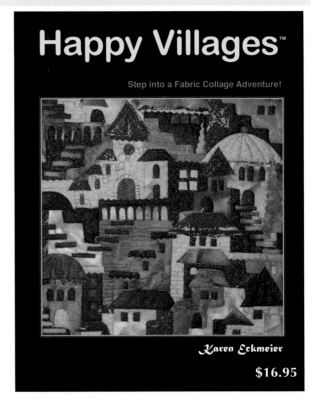

Make more waves and discover the secrets of creating a fabric landscape "accidentally," using Karen's Layered Waves technique. As a complement to her popular Accidental Landscapes pattern series, this guidebook takes you, beginners and seasoned quilters alike, on an inspiring journey to the beloved places in your memories and dreams. You'll find out how to...

o  capture the feeling of a scene in simple layers

o  create a landscape based on a favorite photo, postcard, color palette, memory, or vacation

o  surprise yourself with lively, exciting compositions

o  adopt the same easy techniques for gorgeous, curved borders

Explore the freedom of raw-edge fabric collage! No seams to sew, no points to match, no fusing to gum up your iron.

Fabrics are lightly glue-basted then machine-stitched with a layer of tulle. Step by step, your village magically comes to life.

o  A 16" x 16" project you can create in a day

o  12 variations offered – seasonal, international, whimsical, and more

o  Steps + Rooftops + Windows = Village!

o  Each village you make  is a one-of-a-kind reflection of where you've been, if only in a dream